Best wishes and a Happy Christmas 1990
to Hugh from Harold Davis

Jimmy Wilson.

GLASGOW
RANGERS

PLAYER BY PLAYER

GLASGOW
RANGERS

PLAYER BY PLAYER

Bob Ferrier and Robert McElroy

First published in 1990 by
THE CROWOOD PRESS
Gipsy Lane
Swindon
Wiltshire SN2 6DQ

Text © by BOB FERRIER
Design GRAEME MURDOCH

Photo Acknowledgements:
Colorsport
Glasgow Herald
Syndication International
Sportapics

British Library Cataloguing in Publication Data
Ferrier Bob
Glasgow Rangers : player by player
1. Scotland. Football League football. Clubs, history
I. Title II. McElroy, Robert
796. 3346309411

ISBN 1-85223-404-0

Typeset by Novatext Graphix, Edinburgh.
Printed by BAS Printers Limited, Over Wallop, Hampshire.

INTRODUCTION

Rangers Football Club is a unique institution. There is nothing quite like it anywhere in the world. On all counts, it is the most successful club in Scotland, and one of the oldest, dating from 1872. Its place in the culture of the nation is as distinctive as that of the Church of Scotland, the Scottish legal system, the Royal and Ancient Golf Club of St Andrews. More than any other element in Scottish life, it represents the Protestant, Unionist, Masonic tradition. It has become institutionalised in defence of these things over the years, and its rivalry with the other prominent Glasgow club, Celtic, with its Roman Catholic and Irish origins, cannot be compared with any other football rivalry anywhere in the world. Real Madrid and Barcelona in Spain; AC Milan and Internazionale in Italy; River Plate and Boca Juniors in Argentina, and Penarol and Nacional in Uruguay – there are classic rivals in the world of football, but nowhere else is the rivalry based on religion, as it is with Rangers and Celtic in Scotland.

The traditions which Rangers have maintained have brought the club the support of 'like-minded men' in astonishing numbers, very many of them organised in a supporters-club network which is world-wide. From Shetland to Southampton, from the islands of Lewis and Harris to Liverpool and Leicester and London and Manchester, there are Rangers supporters' clubs. From Lisburn and Londonderry and Armagh in the North of Ireland, the coaches cross on the ferries to Scotland for every Rangers game. There is a Rangers supporters' club in the British Army of the Rhine, another in Hamburg. There is one in Riyadh in Saudi Arabia, where members gather to listen to match broadcasts. In Australia, New Zealand, South Africa, Canada and the USA there are Rangers supporters clubs. Collectively, these clubs represent a remarkable social organism. The football pool which they sustain generates at least £1 million in income for the football club each year, to be used for virtually anything save the purchase of players.

The club's sustained success on the field, and the massive support available to it, has made it seem arrogant in periods of its history. 'We are Rangers – take it or leave it,' has been the creed. And nowhere has this superiority, this self-confidence been made more evident, more manifest, than in the huge main grandstand, built in 1929 when the club was dominating the Scottish game as never before or since. Soaring sixty or seventy feet in the air, seating 10,000 with standing room for a further 9000, its massive red-brick façade is now a listed building. After sixty years of use, the more public areas of this edifice – stairways, seats, roofs – were creaking, rusting and leaking under the stress of time and in 1990 a repair and even rebuilding programme was initiated. This represented the final transformation of Ibrox from the huge, sweeping 'stadium' with a capacity in six figures, almost all standing, to a modern, sophisticated football ground with a capacity of 50,000, all seated. Let us pray they do not seek to transform the private rooms in the old place – the trophy room, the 'cocktail' room, the offices of manager and secretary which enjoy vintage Art-Deco fittings and furnishings.

The transformation of Ibrox has been achieved under the spur of burgeoning European competition, of the prospect of one solitary, open European market and community in 1992, and of the extension and immense financial power of international televised sport. Yet no matter how grand, even grandiose, the stadium, no matter the financial investment in salaries and transfer fees, the game as ever ultimately depends on eleven men on the field, week in, week out, season after season. In the history of Rangers, the club has been blessed with outstanding players, outstanding teams. And in honesty, it has had indifferent players, unsuccessful teams. This book is an attempt to record all the players who have played for the club since the Second World War, more specifically since the start of season 1946–47, to the end of season 1989–90. Our statistics embrace only League Championship, Scottish Cup and League Cup matches, and European competition games. We have ignored friendly matches and those of lesser, local competitions. In a very few instances this includes players who were also at the club before the war. The numbers of international caps include matches played in Italy in the 1990 World Cup Finals. In a couple of cases information is unavailable for international caps won while playing for clubs other than Rangers.

A high proportion of the players listed have played only one game, or a games total in single figures – the wastage at Ibrox has seemed high. But then the wastage in professional football in general is very high, and Rangers probably attract more players, and have first choice of more young players, than any other Scottish club. Many excellent players have been crowded out at Ibrox by simply being there at the wrong time, when there has been a glut of competition for their position, and many have gone on to carve very long and successful careers with other clubs. Examples which come to mind are Alec Scott and Billy Stevenson.

We much appreciate the assistance we have had from Bill Richardson of the Scottish Football Association, David Thomson of the Scottish Football League, journalists Douglas Baillie and Allan Herron, and former Rangers captain Ian McColl. We also acknowledge the invaluable assistance of the 'Rangers Historian' magazine – the definitive club history.

Bob Ferrier
Robert McElroy

LIST OF PLAYERS

ALEXANDER, T.	99	DRINKELL, K.	150	JACKSON, C.	81
ANDERSON, S.	63	DUNCAN, G.	52	JARDINE, W.	85
ARMOUR, D.	108	DUNCANSON, J.	18	JOHANSEN, K.	77
ARNISON, N.	40	DUNLOP, R.	31	JOHNSON, J.	27
ARNISON, W.	19	DURRANT, I.	134	JOHNSTON, M.	152
AUSTIN, A.	52			JOHNSTON, W.	78
		ELLIOTT, A.	48	JOHNSTONE, D.	103
BAILLIE, D.	63				
BAIRD, S.	40	FALCO, M.	147	KENNEDY, A.	126
BARTRAM, J.	148	FERGUSON, A.	89	KENNEDY, S.	109
BAXTER, J.	65	FERGUSON, D.	130	KING, R.	72
BEATTIE, S.	135	FERGUSON, E.	128	KIRKWOOD, D.	143
BECK, T.	80	FERGUSON, IAIN	130	KITCHENBRAND, D.	44
BECKETT, W.	31	FERGUSON, IAN	149		
BELL, D.	135	FINDLAY, W.	25	LIDDELL, C.	34
BETT, J.	119	FLECK, R.	129	LINDSAY, J.	25
BLACK, K.	121	FORREST, J.	73	LITTLE, A.	26
BONNYMAN, P.	105	FORSYTH, A.	118	LITTLE J.	31
BOYD, G.	108	FORSYTH, T.	104	LOGIE, W.	48
BOYD, W.	34	FRAME, J.	27	LYALL, K.	123
BRAND, R.	42	FRANCIS, T.	149		
BROWN, J.	147	FRANKS, A.	62	MACDONALD, A.	92
BROWN, R.	8	FRASER, C.	131	MACDONALD, I.	95
BRUCE, A.	126	FRASER, S.	129	MACDONALD, J.	120
BURNS, H.	131	FYFE, G.	98	MACDONALD, K.	151
BUTCHER, T.	138			MACFARLANE, D.	135
		GARDINER, W.	34	McADAM, C.	120
CALDOW, E.	36	GILLICK, T.	16	McCALL, I.	146
CASKIE, J.	18	GINSBERG, BEN Z.	153	McCALLUM, A.	99
CHRISTIE, J.	72	GOUGH, R.	144	McCLELLAND, J.	121
CLARK, R.	118	GRAY, A.	151	McCLOY, P.	97
CLARK, S.	126	GRAY, D.	18	McCOIST, A.	132
COHEN, A.	143	GRANT, R.	63	McCOLL, I.	22
CONN, A.	94	GREIG, J.	70	McCULLOCH, W.	30
COOPER, D.	116	GRIERSON, D.	35	McDOUGALL, I.	108
COOPER, N.	150			McEWAN, A.	54
COWAN, T.	150	HAMILTON, J.	105	McGREGOR, J.	146
COX, S.	10	HENDERSON, M.	108	McINTYRE, JOHN	30
CUNNING, R.	40	HENDERSON, W.	68	McINTYRE, JAMES	121
		HERON, B.	94	McKEAN, R.	110
DALZIEL, G.	118	HOGG, W.	54	McKENZIE, GEORGE	35
DAVIES, B.	123	HOUSTON, D.	105	McKENZIE, GORDON	35
DAVIS, H.	49	HUBBARD, J.	27	McKINNON, D.	127
DAWSON, A.	111	HUME, R.	62	McKINNON, R.	67
DENNY, J.	99	HUNTER, D.	108	McLEAN, G. (1)	62
DODDS, D.	153	HUNTER, W.	72	McLEAN, G. (2)	62
DONALDSON, G.	104	HYND, R.	75	McLEAN, T.	106

LIST OF PLAYERS

McMinn, K.	134	Pryde, W.	34	Strickland, D.	114
McMillan, H.	35	Prytz, R.	124	Symon, S.	10
McMillan, I.	57	Provan, D.	58		
McNee, C.	26			Telfer, W.	53
McPhee, W.	94	Queen, J.	48	Thomson, A.	48
McPherson, D.	125			Thornton, W.	17
McPherson, J.	27	Rae, W.	24	Traill, D.	72
McSwegan, G.	146	Redford, I.	118		
Mackay, W.	114	Reid, A.	72	Urquhart, W.	114
Martin, N.	60	Ritchie, W.	46		
Marshall, D.	26	Roberts, G.	142	Valentine, J.	52
Mason, J.	105	Robertson, C.	112	Vinnicombe, C.	153
Mathieson, W.	76	Robertson, D.	123		
Matthew, A.	55	Robertson, S.	151	Waddell, W.	14
Melrose, H.	54	Robertson, T.	54	Walker, J.	40
Menzies, R.	35	Rodger, J.	35	Walker, N.	128
Millar, J.	41	Russell, R.	113	Walmsley, W.	27
Miller, A.	101	Rutherford, E.	24	Walters, M.	146
Miller, C.	135			Watkins, C.	10
Mitchell, D.	126	Scott, Alex	39	Watson, C.	72
Moles, W.	52	Scott, Ally	108	Watson, K. (1)	95
Morris, E.	105	Semple, W.	88	Watson, K. (2)	112
Morrison, R.	52	Setterington, D.	80	Watson, R.	80
Munro, I.	112	Sharp, R.	108	Watson, R.M.	99
Munro, S.	129	Shaw, Jock	11	West, C.	136
Murray, M.	40	Shaw, John	25	White, W.	95
		Shearer, R.	45	Wilkins, R.	145
Neef, G.	93	Simpson, R.	31	Williamson, R.	128
Neillands, I.	34	Simpson, W.	28	Williamson, W.	19
Nicholl, J.	127	Smith, A.	83	Willougby, A.	74
Nisbet, S.	136	Smith, D.	82	Wilson, D.	50
Niven, G.	32	Smith, G.	114	Wood, W.	76
		Smith, W.	52	Woodburn, W.	21
O'Hara, A.	105	Sorensen, E.	86	Woods, C.	132
Orr, R.	55	Sorensen, J.	76	Woods, J.	35
		Souness, G.	140	Woods, N.	143
Parlane, D.	100	Spackman, N.	153		
Parlane, J.	19	Stanners, D.	34	Young, G.	114
Paterson, C.	123	Stead, A.	19	Young, G.L.	13
Paterson, W.	55	Steele, J.	112	Young, Q.	104
Paton, W.	26	Stein, C.	90		
Paul, W.	80	Sterland, M.	150		
Penman, A.	88	Steven, T.	151		
Penman, W.	143	Stevens, Gary	148		
Persson, O.	88	Stevens, Gregor	115		
Phillips, J.	143	Stevenson, W.	55		
Prentice, J.	30	Stewart, J.	122		

BOBBY BROWN
1946–56

Bobby Brown was the Adonis, the golden boy who was the first (or last) line of Rangers' famous 'Iron Curtain' defence in the years immediately after the Second World War. From 1946 until 1952, 'Brown, Young and Shaw' was the inevitable start to any Rangers team selection, followed by a variety of wing-halfs – McColl, Symon, Cox, Rae, Watkins – around the centre-half Woodburn.

Tall, slim, blond and athletic, Bobby Brown moved from Falkirk High School to Queen's Park in 1939 and played his first match for them against Celtic at Parkhead in April 1940, before a crowd of 50,000. The match was drawn, 4–4! Brown served in the Fleet Air Arm during the war and guested for Portsmouth, Plymouth, Chester and Chelsea. In 1945, still an amateur, he became an international player when selected to play against England on 5 February at Villa Park. Young Brown faced a forward line that included Matthews, Lawton and Mortensen, a defence that included Swift, Hardwicke, Franklin and Mercer. The Scots went down 3–2, but 'Boy' Brown played very well.

With the war over, he enrolled at Jordanhill College in Glasgow to train as a PE teacher. He turned professional and joined Rangers on the same day as Sammy Cox arrived from Dundee, and forty-eight hours later they were both in the team for a Victory Cup match at Airdrie – 3 May 1946. Brown's early days at Ibrox were not all sweetness and light. For one thing, he was succeeding Jerry Dawson, one of Rangers' finest goalkeepers who had been at the club since 1929 and had collected fourteen international caps before the war. Dawson was an outstanding goalkeeper and a lively, outgoing personality, and the Ibrox crowd let Brown know what they expected of him. Then as an amateur turning professional, he had negotiated his own signing fee and terms. The fee was spread over a number of seasons and made him the highest-paid player at Ibrox, which was not calculated to delight some of his more senior team-mates.
Bobby qualified and became a PE teacher at Denny High School, remaining a part-time player throughout his time with Rangers. After a few months, he settled into a golden career with the club. He was a signed player for ten years, although he played infrequently after 1952. In his half-dozen years, an outstanding Rangers team was challenged persistently and successfully not by Celtic, but by the Hibernian team of Gordon Smith and Lawrie Reilly. Bobby Brown left Rangers for Falkirk in May 1956. The transfer fee was £2200. Within a year he had retired from the game, his heart still with Rangers. In his first six seasons at Ibrox he had missed only one League game, and once played in 179 successive matches. Bobby always took the field with brand-new, shining-white laces in his boots.

He became manager of St Johnstone and led them into the top division, and was Scotland team manager from February 1967 until July 1971.

Games:	296
Shutouts:	109
League Championship:	1946–47, 48–49, 49–50
Scottish Cup:	1947–48, 48–49, 49–50
League Cup:	1946–47, 48–49
Honours:	3 Scotland caps
Born:	Dunipace, 19 March 1923

SAMMY COX
1946–55

As beautifully balanced as any footballer who ever played for Rangers and Scotland, Sammy Cox was in a sense a player out of his time. He could well have fitted comfortably into any Brazilian team of the eighties. An Ayrshire boy from Darvel, he played as a teenage amateur during the Second World War with Queen's Park, Third Lanark and Dundee. He joined Rangers as a professional in May 1946, on the same day as goalkeeper Bobby Brown, and like Brown had established himself in the team within a year, playing every League match of season 1947–48. He went on to have an outstanding ten-year career at Ibrox, then played a few more seasons with East Fife before emigrating to Canada in 1959.

Cox was essentially a left-sided player, but he played with distinction in either full-back position, either wing-half position. Indeed, he played an international match against France in Paris in 1948 as an inside-forward. He also captained Scotland against England in the Hampden match of 1954. By the end of the 1940s he was ready to succeed Jock Shaw and became the regular left-back in both Rangers and Scotland teams.

His play was characterised by balance, quickness and a supreme confidence based on his exceptional technical ability. Cox had a sophisticated football brain which, in spite of the fact that he was not quite 5'8" in height and but 150 lb in weight, allowed him to make the most crisp and incisive tackles. His positional and tactical sense led him to base his defensive work on manoeuvring opponents into dead-end locations, and he had particular success against outstanding wingers such as Stanley Matthews and Tom Finney. He was a regular in the Scotland team from 1949 to 1954.

Games:	310
Goals:	18
League Championship:	1948–49, 49–50, 52–53
Scottish Cup:	1947–48, 48–49, 49–50
League Cup:	1948–49
Honours:	24 Scotland caps
Born:	Darvel, 13 April 1924

CHARLIE WATKINS
1946–48

Charlie Watkins, a Glasgow boy, was a right-half, a good, honest, right-footed player who at around 5'9" was strongly built and always very fit. He was already at the club when Ian McColl was signed in 1945, aged eighteen. McColl, who had had two full seasons with Queen's Park, went straight into the team, but quickly discovered that the professional game required some learning and was bundled into the reserves. Watkins played the entire 1945–46 season in the position. He started 1946–47 as the man in possession, but the talented young McColl quickly forced his way into the team and stayed there, going on to have an exceptional Rangers career. Charlie Watkins was hard-working, not over-skilled but a solid club man wholly committed to Rangers. But with McColl and Sammy Cox installed as wing-halfs, he was always going to be a reserve, and in September 1948 he moved on to Luton Town. He was a qualified physiotherapist, and later lived in South Africa.

Games:	13
Goals:	0
Born:	Glasgow

SCOT SYMON
1946–47

If ever the talents, the personality, the character of a footballer could be expressed by his performance in one single match, James Scotland ('Scot') Symon would surely have claimed that match was Rangers *v* Moscow Dynamo, Ibrox, 28 November 1945. A crowd of 90,000 packed the Rangers ground to see the Russian team give a brilliant exhibition of passing skills, speed, finishing power and fitness that had them two up after twenty-five minutes and threatening to run all over Rangers, a quite bewildered team. Yet in a marvellous second-half recovery, Rangers saved the match at 2–2 and finally dominated the play. It was a recovery greatly inspired by Symon's ferocious tackling, the accuracy of his long-distance passing, and above all by his blazing spirit.

Scot Symon was born in Errol, near Perth, and attended Perth Academy, a rugby-playing school, but he became a junior international footballer with Dundee Violet before turning professional with Dundee FC in 1930. He moved to Portsmouth in 1935, came to Rangers in 1938, and retired in 1947. A powerful build made him an uncompromising wing-half and his tackling was often little short of venomous. He played once for Scotland, against Hungary in 1938, and clearly lost many of his best years to the Second World War. He also played cricket for Scotland and was the only man capped by the country at both sports until Andy Goram, the Hibernian and Scotland goalkeeper, played cricket for Scotland against Ireland and the Australians in 1989. Scot Symon retired in 1947 to begin a distinguished managerial career with East Fife, Preston North End and Rangers. (See 'The Managers'.)

Games:	37
Goals:	3
League Championship:	1938–39
Honours:	1 Scotland cap
Born:	Errol, 9 May 1911

JOCK SHAW
1946–53

If for no other reason, John 'Tiger' Shaw will be remembered in the Rangers story for his durability, He was a League Championship and Scottish Cup winner in 1950, at the age of thirty-eight, and was forty-two years old when he finally retired. In view of his playing style, which was uncompromising, this was a tribute to his fitness, sustained over so many years. At 5' 7" Jock was small for a full-back, but his tackling was fast, fierce and fearless, bringing him his nickname, and he was a hard-driving captain for Rangers.

His career began with Airdrie in 1933, when they took him from Glasgow junior football and the Benburb club, and he transferred to Rangers in July 1938 for £2000 (!). He played in all four of Scotland's 1947 international matches, but was succeeded over the next couple of years in the national team by his younger brother David, left-back of Hibernian. Following an extensive Rangers tour in the summer of 1954 to Canada and the USA, Shaw (and Willie Thornton) retired, and Shaw subsequently had a long and successful association with the club as trainer and later groundsman. He had played in two wartime internationals, in 1941 and 1943, both at Hampden and both against England, and in 'Victory' internationals in 1945 and 1946. Indeed, he and his brother David formed the full-back partnership in the 1946 Victory international against England, which Scotland won 1–0.

Games:	238
Goals:	1
League Championship:	1938–39, 46–47, 48–49, 49–50
Scottish Cup:	1947–48, 48–49, 49–50
League Cup:	1946–47, 48–49
Honours:	4 Scotland caps
Born:	Annathill, 29 November 1912

GEORGE YOUNG
1946–57

Dubbed 'Corky' because of the lucky champagne cork he habitually carried, George Lewis Young was a giant in every respect, even in the long list of outstanding Rangers players. At 6'2" and weighing 15 stone, he was a massive man, albeit quite nimble on long, rather spindly legs. A natural centre-half, he played most of his career at right back, yielding the position to Willie Woodburn, an exceptional player at the heart of a Rangers defence enshrined in club lore as the 'Iron Curtain'. Over six seasons, in 180 League matches, it yielded only 180 goals. When Woodburn was suspended *sine die* in September 1954, Young moved back to centre-half and played out his career there.

He played for Scotland a record fifty-three times and played in thirty-four consecutive matches, records since surpassed by Denis Law and Kenny Dalglish among others. He captained Scotland a record forty-eight times. As captain he found himself in a position seldom equalled before and certainly never since in terms of his influence on the team. Because of his close relationship with George Graham (later Sir George), secretary of the Scottish Football Association, Young was left to arrange training sessions, theatre visits, book local transport and the like, and become in effect a surrogate team manager. The world of football was a good deal less sophisticated in those days, of course, and Young carried off all this perfectly well. But there were rumblings of privilege, not to say patronage, and many players, particularly the Anglo-Scots, were convinced that Young had an undue influence on affairs, team selections included. In consequence, the end of his international career was ironic. He perhaps made the mistake of announcing in advance that his last game would be against Spain in Madrid on 26 May 1957. He was not selected. Perhaps the selectors thought he had been just a shade too presumptuous. He never played for Scotland again.

In movement, George Young was rather less than a thoroughbred, having a rather top-heavy look about him, but he was a marvellously effective footballer, dominant in the air and an awesome tackler. With one simple stretch, his length of leg allowed him to salvage many an apparently lost cause.

With a casual swing of his right leg he could hit clearances of fifty or sixty yards, and this became one of Rangers' most effective attacking gambits. Often these would be directed through the inside-right position, into which centre-forward Thornton would drift in anticipation. These clearances, from the deepest defensive positions, time and again would catch the opposition advanced and completely stretched and exposed. And with the speed and strength of Waddell, the outside-right at the end of these Young clearances, Rangers would be into a counter-attack in a very few seconds. Young's clearances, then, became an important element in attack for that Rangers team. He practised them faithfully in training, and was much more technically skilled than his movement and appearance might have suggested.

Young retired in the summer of 1957, and was later manager of Third Lanark for three years.

Games:	428
Goals:	31
League Championship:	1946–47, 48–49, 49–50, 52–53, 55–56, 56–57
Scottish Cup:	1947–48, 48–49, 49–50, 52–53
League Cup:	1946–47, 48–49
Honours:	53 Scotland caps
Born:	Grangemouth, 27 October 1922

WILLIE WADDELL
1946–56

In all the long history of the Rangers club, now well into its second century, no one has made a greater contribution to its development at so many levels than Willie Waddell. From the time he first played for Rangers in a reserve match against Partick Thistle at Firhill, at the age of fifteen in 1936, until he retired in the eighties, Waddell had been player, manager, general manager, managing director/vice chairman, director/consultant and finally an honorary director of the club. All this was over a scarcely interrupted span of some fifty years.

He first went to Ibrox as a schoolboy and manager Struth arranged for him to gain experience with Strathclyde Juniors for a spell. He signed as a professional in May 1938, and played his initial game for the first team on 9 August at Ibrox against Arsenal. Not only that, he scored the only goal of the match. He established himself that season as Rangers' regular outside-right, playing throughout the war so that when Rangers' first great post-war team of the late forties fell into place, Waddell, in his mid twenties, was a seasoned, powerful outside-right.

In action, Willie Waddell was a strangely menacing player. He was strongly built, full in the chest, wide in the shoulder, not over-tall. His upper torso was thrust forward as his stride lengthened and he was alarmingly fast. Exceptional powers of acceleration often brought him pulled thigh muscle injuries. He was particularly skilful in crossing probing balls, many of which found Thornton's head and produced a high proportion of the centre-forward's many goals. Waddell himself was a very powerful finisher. There was intimidation, and huge excitement for the crowds in the very sight of Willie Waddell in full cry, and he was, in addition and in the local vernacular, 'crabbit' and 'carnaptious' with referees, opponents, even team-mates occasionally if they did not conform. To a large extent this attitude persisted throughout his life, and it may have contributed to his later successes.

He was a qualified and talented journalist, working for Glaswegian and national newspapers. He finished playing in the summer of 1956 and a year later became manager of Kilmarnock. He returned to Ibrox in December 1969. (See 'The Managers'.)

Games:	296
Goals:	56
League Championship:	1938–39, 46–47, 48–49, 52–53
Scottish Cup:	1948–49, 52–53
Honours:	17 Scotland caps
Born:	Forth, Lanarkshire, 7 March 1921

TORRY GILLICK
1946–50

A superbly skilful 'old-fashioned' type of inside-forward, Torrance ('Torry') Gillick was unique. He was the only player that Rangers' fabled manager, William Struth, welcomed back to Ibrox a second time, after he had left the club. Gillick, from Airdrie, was playing at the age of fifteen for Petershill, one of the most prominent of Glasgow's junior clubs. Rangers signed him in 1933 before he was eighteen as a winger, and he won a Scottish Cup medal with them in 1935. That same year, rather surprisingly, he was transferred to Everton for £8000, a then-record Everton fee. He played successfully with the Liverpool club until the start of the Second World War, winning five Scotland caps and a Football League Championship medal in 1939 during that time.

He had played for Everton against Rangers at Ibrox in the 1938 Empire Exhibition tournament, then guested for Rangers and Airdrieonians during the war. He was brought back to Ibrox by Struth in 1945, and that year another claim to fame fell to him in the famous Rangers–Moscow Dynamo match. Torry stopped the play to inform the referee that the Russians had twelve players on the field!

Gillick developed into an outstanding forward of impressive ball control and perceptive positional play. In those post-war seasons, in an exceptional Rangers team, he formed a wonderfully effective wing with Willie Waddell, the quality of Gillick's passing being quite superb. From a rather crouching, round-backed posture, he hit and clipped the ball beautifully. He was particularly adept at placing perfectly weighted passes inside the opposing full-back to draw out and maximise Waddell's burning speed and powerful running. He could score goals too – in season 1946–47, for example, he hit twelve in twenty-seven League matches, five in eight League Cup matches. Gillick was heavily set physically, and in motion was certainly not the most beautiful of athletes, but his short strides gave him a crackling burst of speed and acceleration over ten yards.

He was well-loved, in spite of being disputatious on the field. The Glasgow expression 'greetin' face' might be used to describe him as he moaned at everyone – referees, opponents, even his own players. And he had a rather caustic humour. When opponents would say, 'We're on a £50 bonus,' he'd reply, 'We're getting only a tenner, but then we always win our bonuses, you don't.' And when manager Struth decided that Rangers players, to be properly turned out, must wear bowler hats, the story was that Gillick used to carry his in a brown paper bag until he was within sight of Ibrox, then, still reluctantly, put it on his head.

Torry Gillick died, rather prematurely, on 12 December 1971. On that same day, perhaps the most famous of all Rangers players also died. His name was Alan Morton.

Games:	140
Goals:	62
League Championship:	1946–47
Scottish Cup:	1934–35, 1947–48
League Cup:	1946–47, 48–49
Honours:	5 Scotland caps
Born:	Airdrie, 19 May, 1915
Everton	
Football League Championship:	1938–39

WILLIE THORNTON
1946–54

A prodigy of the generation of Waddell and Woodburn, Willie Thornton of Winchburgh Albion in West Lothian signed for Rangers at the age of sixteen, in March 1936. As did Waddell, he played his first match for the club in the reserves, against Partick Thistle at Firhill as an outside-right. He became a professional in March 1937 and in season 1937–38 played in twenty matches. In 1938–39 he established himself in the team, played a total of forty-three matches, and at the age of nineteen won the first of his four Championship medals.

Willie was a stylish, sophisticated and very, very skilful centre-forward, immensely popular with the Rangers fans for the quality of his play and scoring ability, but above all else for his sportsmanship. He was a silky, thoroughbred, left-sided player with a deft touch in his left foot for dummying or fluttering over the ball, and with an exceptional talent in the air. One of the most profitable attacking gambits in that powerful Rangers team of the late forties and early fifties was the Waddell cross to the Thornton head, and a high proportion of Thornton's goals were headed. He was the first of the post-war Rangers forwards to top a hundred League goals (109 from 164 matches), his best season being 1948–49 when he had twenty-three from twenty-nine League games. Rangers won League, League Cup and Scottish Cup that season, the first of their post-war trebles. Perhaps more remarkable was the fact that in his last playing season with the club, 1953–54, he scored eight goals in eight League matches.

Thornton lost precious time during the Second World War, the best part of six years in which he served with the Duke of Atholl's Highlanders and won the Military Medal in the Italian campaign. If there were any criticism of Willie Thornton, even from the bluest-nosed of 'Blue-noses', it might have been that he was too polite, too much of a gentleman to be a vintage Rangers centre-forward. But the length of his career, and its distinction, would reject that. He was Scotland's Player of the Year in 1952, and when he retired in June 1954 he became manager of Dundee FC. He later managed Partick Thistle and became assistant manager at Ibrox to Willie Waddell. He now acts as a host to visitors to Ibrox, and on match days presides in the Thornton Suite.

Games:	303
Goals:	188
League Championship:	1938–39, 46–47, 48–49, 49–50
Scottish Cup:	1947–48, 48–49, 49–50
League Cup:	1946–47, 48–49
Honours:	7 Scotland caps
Born:	Winchburgh, 3 March 1920

JIMMY DUNCANSON
1946–50

An aggressive striker, the red-haired, instantly recognisable Duncanson from Dennistoun was a tremendous worker, ranging up and down the field as an inside-left in the manner of his pre-war predecessor, the famous Bob McPhail. Jimmy was quick and combative, and for Rangers fans his greatest single talent may have been his habit of scoring against Celtic. He formed a menacing strike force with Willie Thornton, Duncanson being equally adept in the air. He quite often headed goals from 18 yards. He was a tall, hardy, straight-backed type of player who occasionally played outside-left. He moved to St Mirren in November 1950 and to Stranraer in 1953 for a couple of final seasons. He remained a fervent Rangers supporter and in his later days was often seen as a spectator at Ibrox. Jimmy scored Rangers' 4000th goal versus Dundee at Dens Park, on Christmas Day, 1947-he scored all three in the 3-1 win.

Games:	140
Goals:	59
League Championship:	1946–47, 48–49
Scottish Cup:	1947–48, 48–49, 49–50
League Cup:	1946–47, 48–49
Honours:	1 Scotland cap
Born:	Glasgow, 13 October 1919.

DAVID GRAY
1946–47

A Dundee man, very fit, very quick, small and stocky, David Gray in one sense was looked on as a possible successor at right-back to Dougie Gray, the Aberdeenshire man who played an astonishing and record 940 games for the club from 1925 to 1946. It was a tall order, and David didn't quite make it. He played nine League games in 1946–47, but George Young took over the position, and held it.

Games:	12
Goals:	0
Born:	Dundee

JIMMY CASKIE
1946–47

Jimmy Caskie from Possilpark was essentially a pre-war and wartime player. A classic 'Glesca man' – small, bow-legged, tricky – he was a very clever player. In wartime international matches he played eight times for Scotland while with St Mirren, usually in his favoured position of outside-left, sometimes at outside-right. In one of those matches against England he beat the famous goalkeeper Frank Swift with a prodigious left-foot shot. He was an elusive, jinking winger with impish dribbling skills, and against Leslie Compton in particular could be uncontainable. He had been at Everton with Torry Gillick in 1945, but like Gillick came to Ibrox and they were both in the Rangers forward line which played in a historic match against Benfica in Lisbon in 1948. Rangers played at home on the Saturday, travelled Sunday, played Tuesday, came home Wednesday. It was thought to be the first mid-week, mid-season international friendly. The Rangers forward line was Waddell, Gillick, Thornton, Duncanson and Caskie, a quintet valued now in the millions of pounds. Rangers won 3–0. In season 1947–48 Jimmy played fifteen times in all, but with Duncanson and Rutherford and a host of younger players on hand, his time at Ibrox came to an end soon afterwards.

Games:	39
Goals:	5
League Championship:	1946–47
Born:	Glasgow

BILLY WILLIAMSON
1946–51

In the annals of the Rangers club, Billy Williamson has a secure, surely unique place. In successive years at Ibrox he played in only two Scottish Cup ties, each time in a final, each time scoring, each time heading his goal, each time on the winning side. In the 1947–48 replay against Morton (seen by a mid-week record crowd of 129,176 at Hampden) he headed the only goal of the match after 115 minutes' play, from an Eddie Rutherford cross. The following year he headed Rangers' second goal in a 4–1 defeat of Clyde. Two games, two winners' medals – hard to beat.

Billy was a stocky, barrel-chested inside- or centre-forward, always on hand if either Thornton or Duncanson was injured. He had been a PE instructor in the Royal Navy during the war, a PE schoolteacher subsequently, and was always tremendously fit, even athletic, often indulging in cartwheels when falling or getting back to his feet. He was transferred to St Mirren on 20 February 1951.

Games:	69
Goals:	39
League Championship:	1949–50
Scottish Cup:	1947–48, 48–49
League Cup:	1946–47
Born:	Glasgow

BILLY ARNISON
1946–49

14
Billy Arnison
1946–49

The first of five South Africans who have played for the club since 1945, Billy from Johannesburg was a powerful centre-forward who never quite established himself at Ibrox, yet had the not unimpressive record of sixteen goals scored in eighteen games. Only 5' 9", he played with vigour and had a strength that saw him play the ball and at the same time remove opponents without ever being particularly dirty. He was transferred to Luton Town on 16 August 1948, for £7000.

Games:	10
Goals:	4
Born:	Johannesburg

ANGUS STEAD
1946–47

An outside-right, small and quick, Angus joined the club in May 1945, but was on military service for most of the next two years.

Games:	4
Goals:	1
Born:	Glasgow

JIMMY PARLANE
1946–48

One of a remarkable footballing family from Rhu in Dunbartonshire, Jimmy at one time had three brothers playing for Dumbarton in the Scottish League. He had three sons, one of whom, Derek, played for Rangers a generation on. Jimmy was a stuffy, hard-working, ball-winning inside-forward who like so many others had lost prime time to the war and who found it hard to crack into that fine Rangers team of the late forties. He went to Airdrie on loan for a spell and enjoyed it so much that he stayed, signing for them on 8 January 1948. Inside-left to his inside-right in that Airdrie team was young Ian McMillan. Jimmy later played for Dumbarton.

Games:	7
Goals:	3
Born:	Helensburgh

WILLIE WOODBURN
1946–55

Perhaps the most gifted centre-half Rangers have ever had, Willie Woodburn is remembered now mainly for the fact that he was suspended *sine die* on 14 September 1954, and although the suspension was lifted on 23 April 1957 he never again played senior football. Indeed, he had effectively left the club in the summer of 1955.

Woodburn simply had too many brushes with authority, all of these emerging from a burning desire to secure victory for Rangers. Defeat seemed to be a personal affront to Woodburn. He would castigate referees, opponents, even his own players, never accepting excuses from anyone. In particular he would abuse his goalkeeper, Bobby Brown, for every goal lost, no matter how unstoppable the shot might have been – in short, a very passionate man, Mr Woodburn.

He was enormously talented, beautifully balanced on either side. Fractionally under six feet in height, he was resolute and commanding in the air and extreme in defence, taking no prisoners. In possession he would forage forward, the ball under complete control, elbows out from his sides, meticulous and imaginative in the weight and accuracy of his passing. Woodburn was a player of the highest class, without any question a quality international player, perfectly comparable to his opposite number on the contemporary international scene – Neil Franklin of Stoke City and England. A measure of Woodburn's adaptability was that manager Struth had used him as a right-half, even an inside-right on occasion, but it was as the central figure in that marvellous defence of Brown, Young and Shaw, McColl, Woodburn and Cox that Willie Woodburn was in his proper setting, at the very centre of things. He had gone to Ibrox almost directly from juvenile football with Edinburgh Ashton, signing as a professional in October 1937.

Games:	325
Goals:	1
League Championship:	1946–47, 48–49, 49–50, 52–53
Scottish Cup:	1947–48, 48–49, 49–50, 52–53
League Cup:	1946–47, 48–49
Honours:	24 Scotland caps
Born:	Edinburgh, 8 August 1919

IAN McCOLL (JOHN MILLER McCOLL)
1946–61

Ian McColl vies with, say, John Greig in having the ultimate career, with thirteen League and Cup successes in fifteen years with Rangers. In addition, there were fourteen appearances for Scotland, more than four thoroughly enjoyable years as Scotland team manager, followed by almost three years as manager of Sunderland in the English First Division. Thus a youthful promise was handsomely fulfilled.

Ian was a flinty wing-half from Vale of Leven, in its time a famous forcing ground for footballers, and after local school and Boys' Brigade football, was playing with Queen's Park when he was sixteen. He was signed by Rangers before he was eighteen in June 1945, and after half a season or so in the reserves to acclimatise him to the world of the professionals, he was in the 'big' team, with Young behind him, Woodburn to his left, Waddell and Thornton in front – reasonable tutors for a young man. They were accustomed to winning; they were in a winning team, and McColl was quickly infected by the fever.

He was tall, very athletic, a powerful tackler and ball-winner who would fight for every ball and battle throughout the entire match with a hard quality in his play, comparable to the style of one of his predecessors, Scot Symon. Both were very vigorous players who took no prisoners, yet both were gifted in their use of the ball. Manager Struth at times rebuked McColl for 'taking two bites at the cherry', in bringing the ball under instant control. McColl came to realise, rather quickly in that company, that playing for Rangers was rather special, that the expectation was very much higher and the demands more exacting at Ibrox than anywhere else, and he became a perfectionist, a hard-driving taskmaster and an inspirational player and captain of the club.

He took this pragmatic attitude into management with Scotland, and in his later business life. With sixteen victories in twenty-seven matches, he is probably the most successful national team manager, but points out that in his time, he could call on Crerand and Law from Manchester United, Brown, Mackay and White from Tottenham Hotspur, and Caldow, Baxter, Henderson and Wilson from Rangers.

Games:	526
Goals:	14
League Championship:	1946–47, 48–49, 49–50, 52–53, 55–56, 56–57
Scottish Cup:	1947–48, 48–49, 49–50, 52–53, 59–60
League Cup:	1946–47, 48–49
Honours:	14 Scotland caps
Born:	Alexandria, 7 June 1927

WILLIE RAE
1946–57

A strong, industrious left-side player, mainly in the left-half position, Willie Rae had a decade at Ibrox in which he was in the main a reserve to McColl and Cox, players who could be dispossessed only by injury. He was always a part-time player and became a qualified quantity surveyor, moving to Queen of the South – there were family connections in Dumfries.

Games:	179
Goals:	7
League Championship:	1946–47, 55-56
Scottish Cup:	1949–50
League Cup:	1946–47
Born:	Glasgow

EDDIE RUTHERFORD
1946–52

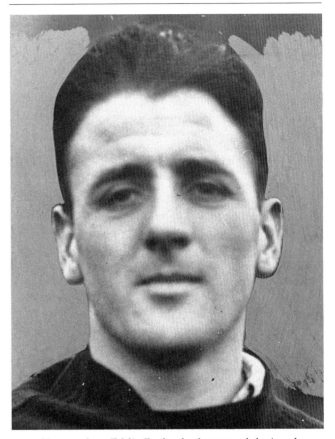

A Glasgow boy, Eddie Rutherford emerged during the Second World War when, having signed for Rangers in August 1941, he guested for Lincoln City and Bradford City. He was a natural outside-right, but with the war over, with Willie Waddell firmly in place there and with Jimmy Caskie's career coming to an end, Eddie became the regular outside-left. Slim and quick, Eddie sometimes looked uncomfortable in the position, but he was well served by such wing-halfs as Sammy Cox and Willie Rae and by inside-left Jimmy Duncanson, and was an effective member of the team, particularly dangerous when he cut inside on to his right foot. Eddie, even in temperament, always seemed to enjoy it all. After ten years with Rangers he was exchanged for Colin Liddell of Hearts on 9 November 1951. He later played for Raith Rovers, then Hamilton Academicals, before retiring in 1956.

Games:	140
Goals:	28
League Championship:	1948–49, 49–50
Scottish Cup:	1947–48, 48–49, 49–50
League Cup:	1946–47, 48–49
Honours	1 Scotland cap
Born:	Glasgow, 8 February 1921

JOHN LINDSAY
1946–52

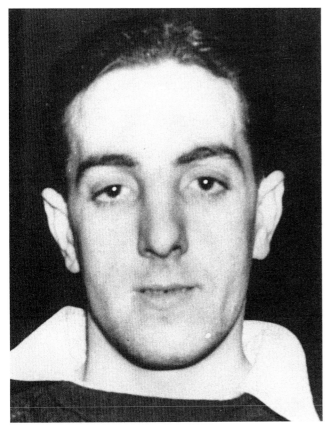

John was an elegant, stylish full-back, brought to Ibrox to be the successor to Jock Shaw, to play in the reserves until the time came. It never did. Shaw went on playing into his forty-second year, by which time John Little had appeared from Queen's Park. The few chances Lindsay did have showed that so much reserve football had done nothing for his pace and sharpness. However, he did move on to Everton where he had several successful seasons.

Games:	22
Goals:	0
Born:	Glasgow

JOHN SHAW
1946–47

John Shaw, reserve goalkeeper, had much the same experience as John Lindsay. With Bobby Brown in place at Ibrox, he had only one match, a League Cup tie at Cappielow against Morton, with Rangers won 2–0.

Games:	1
Shutouts:	1
Born:	Glasgow

WILLIE FINDLAY
1947–54

Willie Findlay was signed from Albion Rovers in the summer of 1947 with the thought that he should succeed Torry Gillick. He was known as 'Banana Findlay' because every pass he played seemed to have a 'bend' on it. He was tall, rather slim, not perhaps the greatest worker Rangers ever had, but a keen and persistent penalty-area player. Willie's whole desire seemed to be to score goals, and he had a talent for finding good scoring positions in the penalty area. He scored the first of Rangers' goals in their 3–0 Scottish Cup Final win over East Fife in 1950 with a flying header – in just thirty seconds!

Although he was far from being a physical player, he could snap up defensive blunders without fear. He served Willie Waddell well on the wing, and yet always seemed to be on hand when the Waddell crosses came in. In December 1954 he went back to Albion Rovers. There was no fee involved.

Games:	114
Goals:	65
League Championship:	1949–50
Scottish Cup:	1949–50
Born:	Motherwell

CHRIS McNEE
1946–47

An outside-left from Hamilton Accies, Chris was a bright and clever winger who had lost good years to the war.

Games: 10
Goals: 3
Born: Glasgow

WILLIE PATON
1947–57

Willie Paton, a contemporary of Willie Findlay, was a rather stronger player, an inside-forward of strength and stamina.
From Petershill Juniors in the Springburn district of Glasgow, he was well suited to the dictum of the manager, Bill Struth, and indeed that of his successor, Scot Symon – inside-forwards should be the workhorses of the team. Many critics claimed that if Willie had been less modest, less polite, less of a gentleman, he would have had a more forceful career at Ibrox. On 21 September 1956 he moved to Ayr United for a token £1000 fee.

Games: 165
Goals: 65
League Championship: 1948–49
Scottish Cup: 1952–53
League Cup: 1948–49
Born: Glasgow

DAVID MARSHALL
1946–53

A very skilful inside-forward, one of the most able ball players at the club during his time there, but perhaps a little short of work rate, illustrating that one of the major requirements for success with Rangers is to play flat out in every match, sustaining form and effort through the entire ninety minutes. David was given a free transfer on 2 May 1953.

Games: 20
Goals: 9
Born: Glasgow

ADAM LITTLE
1947–52

Yet another fine player who was robbed of vintage years by the Second World War, Adam from Rutherglen was a product of Queen's Park. He was a stylish wing-half, light on his feet, a thinking player who used the ball with accuracy and imagination. He had been with Rangers since 1937, and during the war from time to time featured in a Little–Young–Simon half-back line. He won a wartime cap for Scotland against England at Maine Road, Manchester on 16 October 1943 and probably wished he hadn't – Scotland lost 8–0. He guested for Arsenal during the war, and finally left Rangers for Morton on 3 July 1951 on a free transfer. Little had qualified as a doctor and he was in general practice for many years.

Games: 6
Goals: 0
Born: Rutherglen

JOE JOHNSON
1947–52

A physical education teacher from the Renfrew–Paisley area, Joe was a big, strong, fast, straight-running inside- or outside-left, a good worker but not perhaps the most subtle player Rangers ever had. He was transferred to Falkirk on 8 November 1951 and later went to live in Vancouver, Canada. Joe was known as 'Farmer Joe'.

Games: 36
Goals: 14
League Championship: 1949–50
Born: Greenock

IAN (JOHN) McPHERSON
1947–48

A small, stocky inside-forward who came from Troon Juniors in June 1947.

Games: 1
Goals: 1
Born: Glasgow

JIMMY FRAME
1948–52

An outside-right, he joined Rangers from Clydebank Juniors in May 1948. He was a winger, rather small, with close ball control. He played one League game, against Dundee on 28 August 1948, but was freed at the end of season 1951–52, having been on National Service for much of his time at Ibrox. He moved on to Dumbarton.

Games: 1
Goals: 0
Born: Clydebank

WILLIE WALMSLEY
1948–49

An outside-left from Clydebank Juniors, Willie came in for the odd game but could not sustain any challenge to the wingers Waddell, Caskie and Rutherford and remained a reserve player.

Games: 1
Goals: 0
Born: Kilmarnock

JOHNNY HUBBARD
1949–59

Johnny Hubbard arrived at Ibrox from South Africa in July 1949. He had been recommended to Rangers by the former Hibernian player Alex Prior, who was then a photographer in South Africa and who had described Hubbard as 'the best player in the Union'. In all the years he spent at Ibrox, the South African, who was only 5' 4" tall, never weighed more than 8 st 10 lb. This fragile, elfin figure was far from looking the part, and at first sight the Rangers manager, Bill Struth, had severe reservations about Johnny. Hubbard's skill with the ball, in running, crossing, shooting and above all dribbling, soon convinced him. Johnny was immensely popular with the Ibrox crowd, which dearly loves tricky wingers. Above all, Hubbard is remembered by older Rangers fans as the penalty-kick king. He converted a phenomenal fifty-four out of fifty-seven penalty-kicks, including twenty-three successive scores from 1949 until 28 January 1956, when he failed against Davie Walker, the Airdrie goalkeeper. Hubbard did score in the match, however, a 4–0 Rangers win with a hat-trick going to Sammy Baird.

Other goalkeepers who achieved a modest immortality in stopping Hubbard penalty shots were Jimmy Brown of Kilmarnock and Bert Slater of Falkirk. John was transferred to Bury on 16 April 1959 for £6000. He returned to Scotland when he had finished playing and became a recreation officer in the Prestwick area of Ayrshire.

Games: 238
Goals: 104
League Championship: 1952–53, 55–56, 56–57
Scottish Cup: 1952–53
Honours: 1 South Africa cap (v Scotland!)
Born: Pretoria

BILLY SIMPSON
1950–59

With the Rangers careers of Torry Gillick, Jimmy Duncanson and Billy Williamson drawing to a close at the end of the decade of the forties, the club badly needed to strengthen its inside-forward 'staff'. Many were tried, many found lacking the standards Rangers required. When a Linfield forward was recommended to the club, manager Struth sent Gillick to Belfast to assess him. Gillick reported favourably, and the result was that on 19 October 1950 Struth paid Linfield £11,500 for Billy Simpson. It was a club record fee, but as good a buy, pound for pound, as Struth ever made. Simpson turned out to be one of a handful of players to score a hundred League goals since 1945.

He played all three inside-forward positions at different times with success. Ian McColl, for instance, enjoyed playing behind him when he was at inside-right, saying 'We read each other well,' but Simpson most often played centre-forward. He was not one of the most physical players you could imagine, not powerful in the slightest. And there was not much style about his work, such as Thornton, for example, possessed. But if he lacked polish, Billy had courage to spare. He was above all a goal-scorer, and he would risk injury to reach that ball, adept as he was in picking up chances and half-chances in the goal area.

One thing he did have in common with Willie Thornton, whom he eventually succeeded, was that he was a magnificent header of the ball and would often dive headlong to head crosses other players would not attempt to reach. His first goals for the club came on Christmas Eve 1950, a hat-trick against East Fife. His hundredth goal was a typical flying header, against Hearts on 26 October 1957. Billy scored four goals no fewer than three times, *v* Third Lanark on 25 April 1951, *v* St Mirren on 20 December 1952 and against Hibs on 1 November 1956.

His single most important goal for Rangers may well have been with his head against Hearts at Tynecastle on 13 April 1957. It broke the Edinburgh team and set up Rangers' Championship after they had been seven points behind Hearts in the final straight. Billy Simpson was many times an Irish international player. In November 1957, he scored the winning goal for Northern Ireland against England at Wembley (2-3), a rare achievement for an Irishman. He joined Stirling Albion on 3 March 1958.

Games:	239
Goals:	165
League Championship:	1952–53, 55–56, 56–57
Scottish Cup:	1952–53
Honours:	12 Ireland caps (all with Rangers)
Born:	Belfast

WILLIE McCULLOCH
1949–55

From the same junior team, Strathclyde Juniors, Willie was reckoned to be in the same mould as Willie Waddell and an ideal successor in age and style. Alas, it never did happen – McCulloch may have been distracted by his other career as a chartered accountant, for which he trained in the practice of Jimmy Simpson, the Rangers club secretary. He became an accountant with Alexandra Transport while still playing, and later went to the company's head office in Scarborough, where he worked and sadly died before he was fifty.

Games: 68
Goals: 15
Born: Glasgow

IAN (JOHN) McINTYRE
1949–55

Another schoolboy star outside-right – manager Bill Struth thought he would be something special, but he didn't make the breakthrough. He moved on to Airdrie, but was always a part-time player. He became a very successful artist with Beaverbrook Newspapers.

Games: 2
Goals: 0
Born: Glasgow

JOHN PRENTICE
1950–56

Transferred from Hearts on 9 March 1950 for £7000, John Prentice was an altogether fine footballer. He was strong and powerful, worked the ball well, particularly with his left foot, and played equally well at left-half or inside-left, where he formed a potent wing partnership with Johnny Hubbard. John was big and fast, and a deep thinker on the game, its problems and its challenges. He was transferred to Falkirk on 18 September 1956 for £2500 and that same season captained Falkirk to a Scottish Cup victory over Kilmarnock. Prentice went on to become a coach, and indeed had a successful spell as manager with Clyde. Jim McLean, the manager of Dundee United and the longest-serving in the game, claims Prentice as the biggest single influence on his career, saying that everything he knows about coaching he learned from Prentice.

In the sixties John became Scotland's team manager for a few months. Even before his terms had been settled, he went to Canada for a job interview without mentioning this to the SFA selection committee. They thought this was less than discreet, and John was invited to move on.

Games: 142
Goals: 36
League Championship: 1952–53
Born: Shotts

Falkirk
Scottish Cup: 1956-57

BOBBY SIMPSON
1950–51

When Bobby Simpson, an inside-right, arrived at Ibrox from the Fife coalfield, he was being compared to Billy Steel! He certainly was the same height, weight, was small and stocky and very, very strong. Alas, Bobby was also rather slow, and never did break through the queue of inside-forwards lining up for places in the Rangers team of the time. He eventually went back to work in the coalfields.

Games:	2
Goals:	2
Born:	Hill o' Beath, Fife

REX DUNLOP
1950–53

A wing-forward, 'Big Rex' made little impression at Ibrox.

Games:	3
Goals:	0
Born:	Dumfries

WILLIAM BECKETT
1950–51

An outside-left who played only one game, against Clyde on 10 March 1951. Rangers won 4–0.

Games:	1
Goals:	0
Born:	Dumbarton

JOHN LITTLE
1950–61

Yet another of Queen's Park's contributions to the Rangers story. John was born in Calgary in Canada, but came to Scotland as a boy. His first school was rugby-playing, but he started to play football at Queen's Park Senior Secondary, a famous football nursery, and became a schoolboy international player and an amateur international after having joined, inevitably, Queen's Park. He became a professional with Rangers in July 1951 and there have been few better investments on the part of any Rangers management. Johnny Little was the perfect successor to Jock Shaw at left-back. Where the elegance of John Lindsay had failed, the sheer speed, energy and exuberance of Little succeeded with a vengeance and Rangers were secure in the position for a decade, after the long years of the immensely durable Jock Shaw. In fact, there was a substantial likeness in playing styles and attitudes between Shaw and Little. Few wingers could get past Johnny and when they did, he invariably caught them. He was an all-action type with much style and effective distribution and his tackling had much of Shaw's tigerish quality.

Little's charm and even temperament made him one of the best-loved players in the game. He was a qualified PE teacher, and he moved to Morton in the summer of 1962 and eventually taught in a school in Greenock. John Little, Colin Jackson and Richard Gough are the only Rangers players to have been capped for Scotland who were born outside the country.

Games:	275
Goals:	1
League Championship:	1952–53, 55–56
Scottish Cup:	1952–53, 59–60
Honours:	1 Scotland cap
Born:	Calgary, 7 July 1930

GEORGE NIVEN
1951–61

In the opening match of season 1952–53, Rangers went to Tynecastle and were trounced 5–0 by Hearts. In the Rangers goal, for the last time, was Bobby Brown. George Niven was his successor, not so dapper, not so striking in appearance as Brown but dependable and courageous. In the 1953 Cup Final, against Aberdeen, he suffered a head injury in going down at the feet of Paddy Buckley after twenty-seven minutes. George Young took his place in goal, but Niven appeared for the second half, his head swathed in bandages, to make a series of magnificent saves which held Aberdeen to a drawn game. Rangers won the replay.

George was on the small side for a goalkeeper, but was thoroughly reliable over a good many seasons at Ibrox. Like most keepers, he had good days and bad days, the worst of them being perhaps the 1957 League Cup Final when Celtic won 7–1, prompting the unsubtle Celtic joke 'What's the time? Seven past Niven.' George had made his debut in fact in the last match of 1951–52, a 1–1 draw with Aberdeen at Pittodrie, and his best season was perhaps 1959-60 when he was outstanding and was selected to play for Scotland against England. Injury in the Scottish Cup semi-final against Celtic caused him to withdraw. It was his only Scottish selection. Billy Ritchie played in that semi-final replay, but Niven was back for the final in a Rangers team which beat Kilmarnock 2–0.

George played his last match for Rangers against Motherwell at Ibrox on 25 March 1961, a 2–2 draw, and moved on to Partick Thistle in February of the following year. There, he played on with distinction in what was one of Thistle's best-ever teams.

Games:	327
Shutouts:	106
League Championship:	1952–53, 55–56, 56–57, 58–59, 60–61
Scottish Cup:	1952–53, 59–60
League Cup:	1960–61
Born:	Blairhall

COLIN LIDDELL
1951–55

Yet another Queen's Park product, Colin reached Rangers by way of Hearts, when he was exchanged for Eddie Rutherford on 9 November 1951, and effectively kept Johnny Hubbard out of the team for the rest of that season. The situation was reversed in 1952–53, when Colin managed only six League games. He was tall, strong and hard-running at outside-left, a product of Albert Senior Secondary School in Springburn, Glasgow. Colin was no relation to his famous contemporary Billy Liddell of Liverpool and Scotland. They were similar in build and type, but Colin did not have the same success in scoring goals. He moved on to Morton, where he had a reasonably lengthy career.

Games: 52
Goals: 12
Born: Glasgow

WILLIE PRYDE
1951–56

Willie, a strong, hard-working left-half, always a reserve player, had his moments of glory in the Scottish Cup Final of 1953 when he took the place of the injured Sammy Cox in the Rangers teams against Aberdeen – 1–1 and 1–0 in the replay. When he was given a free transfer on 28 April 1956 he was in good company, that of Cox and Willie Waddell among others.

Games: 13
Goals: 0
Scottish Cup: 1952–53
Born: Leuchars, Fife

WILLIE GARDINER
1951–55

Willie, a 6' 3" beanpole from the Dunfermline area, was a scoring centre-forward with a very successful Bo'ness United junior team. He was signed in November 1950 – tall, blond, busy, good turn of speed – but unfortunately the goals did not come as easily or as often for Rangers as they had in junior football. In contention for the centre-forward position in Willie's time at Ibrox were such names as Thornton, Simpson, Grierson, Paton. He moved to Leicester City on 11 August 1955.

Games: 31
Goals: 19
Born: Larbert

DUNCAN STANNERS
1951–56

Events and personalities at Ibrox combined to compromise yet another Rangers career. Duncan, 6'2" tall and a perfectly good centre-half, was an understudy to Young and Woodburn in the fifties and as a result rarely played in the League team. When Woodburn was suspended, Duncan should have filled the place, but probably found that too many seasons in reserve football had stolen his sharpness. George Young moved to centre-half, Eric Caldow became right-back and Duncan moved on to Stirling Albion on 15 December 1955.

Games: 23
Goals: 0
Born: Denny

WILLIE BOYD
1951–52

Boyd was a close friend of Willie McCulloch. Both were at the club at the same time, and both trained as chartered accountants in the office of Jimmy Simpson, the club secretary. He played twice, as inside-right to Willie Waddell, in March 1952, a 5–1 win at Stirling Albion, and a home win over Morton by 1–0. Neillands followed him, but the regular inside-forwards at the time were Paton and Findlay.

Games: 2
Goals: 0
Born: Glasgow

IAN NEILLANDS
1951–56

Ian was a good player not quite up to the demands of being a permanent right-wing partner to Willie Waddell. He joined the club in September 1951 and played three games in March and April of 1952, in what was a barren season for Rangers. All three matches were drawn. Ian was released on 28 April 1956.

Games;   7
Goals: 1
Born: Edinburgh

DEREK GRIERSON
1952–57

.Signed from Queen's Park on 5 August 1952, Derek went straight into the team at inside-right and played in every one of the League matches that season, scoring thirty League goals. He was small but strongly built and quick, clever on the ball, a prime striking forward with a highly developed positional strength. He would probably have conceded that he was not over-industrious in the outfield, doing all his work on rather than off the ball, but he was very dangerous in the penalty area, taking up menacing shooting positions as though by instinct. On 10 January 1957 he went to Falkirk in exchange for Bobby Morrison.

Games	106
Goals:	59
League Championship:	1952–53
Scottish Cup:	1952–53
Born:	Prestonpans
Falkirk	
Scottish Cup:	1956-57

HUNTER McMILLAN
1953–56

P.H. McMillan, cousin of Ian, was a wing-half or inside-forward who joined the club in March 1952 and was freed at the end of the 1955–56 season. He played (scoring Rangers' only goal!) in the 1953 Coronation Cup match against Manchester United (1–2). He later played with Queen of the South and Falkirk and at one time was physiotherapist to the Arbroath club.

Games:	8
Goals:	2
Born:	Glasgow

JOHNNY WOODS
1954–55

A red-haired inside-left, Johnny was a very good player who could not sustain his skills. He was freed on 28 April 1956.

Games:	1
Goals:	0
Born:	Glasgow

JIM RODGER
1953–55

Outside-right. Tall, leggy, and a schoolmaster. He was freed on 19 May 1955, and won a Scottish Cup medal with St Mirren when they beat Aberdeen 3–1 in the 1959 final. He later became a headmaster in the Western Isles.

Games:	3
Goals:	0
Born:	Cleland

GEORGE McKENZIE
1954–55

George was a right-half or centre-half who was freed on 19 May 1955.

Games:	3
Goals:	0
Born:	Leith

GORDON McKENZIE
1954–55

Gordon was 6'3" tall, straight as a Guardsman, a lovely man and a fine left-back with a strong left foot. But as George McKenzie suffered from the presence of Ian McColl, so Eric Caldow kept Gordon out of things. Both McKenzies were freed on 19 May 1955.

Games:	9
Goals:	0
Born:	Glasgow

ROSS MENZIES
1954–55

Ross Menzies' only game was an important one, a League Cup quarter-final match which Rangers lost 1–2 at Motherwell. Bobby Cunning made one of his rare appearances in the team in that same match. Ross had been a flight-lieutenant and PE instructor in the RAF, and became manager of Bishopbriggs Sports Centre.

Games	1
Goals:	0
Born:	Rutherglen

ERIC CALDOW
1953–66

Of all the players who have served the Rangers club, Eric Caldow holds a rare distinction. He has been a member of not one but two of Rangers' greatest teams, the immediate post-war team of the late forties and early fifties, and the team of the early sixties, possibly the best Rangers team of the past fifty years. In his very first match, a League Cup tie against Ayr United at Ibrox in September 1953, Caldow found McColl, Woodburn, Cox and Waddell lining up with him (George Young, his idol, was injured). In his last match at Falkirk in March 1966, the team included Greig, McKinnon, Henderson and Johnston.

Eric Caldow had an outstanding career in which he captained both Rangers and Scotland. He won all the honours. Having played in the earliest European matches, he captained the club in its first European final, the Cup Winners' Cup of 1961 against Fiorentina. He played forty times for Scotland, an international tally that would have been greatly increased but for a vicious tackle he suffered from Bobby Smith, the Tottenham Hotspur centre-forward, after only six minutes of the England–Scotland match at Wembley in 1963. Caldow's left leg was broken in three places. Denis Law told him much later that Smith, a very physical player, had boasted to him before the match that Scotland would finish with only ten men!

Six months later Caldow was able to play reserve football, but managed only three League matches that season. His international career, which would surely have taken him close to George Young's Rangers record of fifty-three caps had it continued, was over. From April 1957 to April 1963 he had missed only two international matches, and had been captain of Scotland for three years. He played a full League season in 1964–65, but the great Rangers team that Scot Symon had put together broke up. His full-back partner Bobby Shearer had been given a free transfer. Ian McMillan moved back to Airdrie, Ralph Brand moved to Manchester City, Jim Baxter to Sunderland. Eric was given a free transfer in April 1966.

Eric Caldow's strength as a full-back lay in his pace. He was very, very quick, and if the best of wingers did get past him, they never could get away from him. He was not a physical player, not over-big at 5' 8" and around 155 lb. In his balance, in the positive nature of his tackling and his adaptability, he was a latter-day Sammy Cox. He played twenty-nine times for Scotland at left-back, eleven times at right-back. His technique was excellent, his tactical thinking in defence that of manoeuvring his winger until the time was exactly right for a crisp tackle. He was a phlegmatic character; nothing seemed to upset Caldow and his captaincy of both Rangers and Scotland was one of example, not of exhortation. In fact, he was never once booked in his long career.

From Cumnock in Ayrshire, Eric had been committed to Rangers from the age of fourteen, when he was playing in schools and youth-club football. It was said that a local schoolteacher, Alex Sloan, a friend of Rangers director George Brown, recommended him to the club. Rangers farmed the boy out to Muirkirk Juniors for a couple of seasons before calling him to Ibrox in 1952. Within a year he was in the team, and within two years he was established in one of the great Rangers careers. After leaving the club fourteen years on, he had a year at Stirling Albion then retired as a player. Ventures in management with Corby Town and Stranraer were not successful. Eric returned to Ibrox in December 1989 to host the new executive facilities with Alec Willoughby.

Games:	407
Goals:	25
League Championship:	1955–56, 56–57, 58–59, 60–61, 62–63
Scottish Cup:	1959–60, 61–62
League Cup:	1960–61, 61–62, 64–65
Honours:	40 Scotland caps
Born:	Cumnock, 14 May 1934

ALEXANDER SILCOCK SCOTT
1954–63

In all the long line of brilliant Rangers wingers, Alex Scott must have an honoured place. He was an outside-right of devastating pace and fearsome finishing power. In his very first match for the club on 9 March 1955, while still a teenager, he scored a hat-trick in a 4–1 win over Falkirk at Ibrox. Six days later he drove in two stunning goals in a 2–2 draw against Arsenal at Highbury.

Alex was the ultimate flying winger, very fast, physically strong at 5' 10" and 12 stone, a good crosser of the ball and a menacing attack force – altogether the perfect replacement for Willie Waddell. From Camelon Thistle in the Falkirk area, he was signed provisionally by Rangers in January 1954 and permanently in March 1955, when he went straight into the team and stayed there for the best part of eight years. He had a rather strange running style because, in spite of his speed, his left arm stayed by his side and scarcely moved.

With the advent of the young, brilliant and quite different Willie Henderson, Scott went to Everton in February 1963 for a fee of £39,000 and as he had done in Scotland with Rangers, won Championship and Cup honours with the Liverpool club. He came back north to Hibs in 1967 and was with Falkirk in the early seventies. As well as full senior internationals, he played for Scotland at Under-23 and B levels. He was in the Rangers team which lost the final of the 1961 European Cup Winners' Cup in Florence, when he scored the only Rangers goal. Indeed, he scored, in all, five goals en route to that final. Alex was the scorer of Rangers' 5000th League goal in the championship-winning game at home to Ayr United, on 29th April, 1961. His younger brother James played for Hibs and for Scotland. They went into business together in Falkirk.

Games:	331
Goals:	108
League Championship:	1955–56, 56–57, 58–59, 60–61
Scottish Cup:	1959–60
League Cup:	1960–61, 61–62
Honours:	16 Scotland caps (11 with Rangers)
Born:	Falkirk, 22 December 1936

Everton
Football League Championship: 1962-63
F.A. Cup: 1965-66

JIMMY WALKER
1956–57

Big, strong, heavily built inside-forward from Clydebank.

Games:	2
Goals:	0
Born:	Stenhousemuir

BOBBY CUNNING
1954–55

Scot Symon paid £2500 to Hamilton Academicals on 2 September 1954 for Bobby Cunning, an outside-left of startling pace, no doubt to add to the wing strength with the departure of Findlay and Rutherford. Bobby, alas, had serious vision problems – he was one of the first footballers to wear contact lenses – and his career was badly compromised.

Games:	5
Goals:	0
Born:	Dunfermline

MAX MURRAY
1955–63

'Slapsie Maxie', as he was called, came from Queen's Park to Rangers with the reputation of being a prolific goal-scorer. An exuberant character, he had but one thought in mind – to hammer that ball at goal, with right foot, left foot or head. And as the records show, although he was essentially a reserve to Jimmy Millar, Max was entirely successful. He was thoroughly reliable, an all-action player who never let the team down. He was tall and slender with very little physical strength, but quick and with a good turn of speed. There was little that was sophisticated about his play and it is true to say that he was not highly popular with all Rangers fans. They thought him cumbersome – he had 'the action of a combine harvester with the brakes off', was one description.

He would slash at balls and blast them over the bar impetuously, when often a simple side-foot would have done. Yet he scored some important goals for the club. In the Scottish Cup semi-final of 1962, in place of Millar, he scored two of the Rangers goals in a 3–1 win over Motherwell. Max was transferred to West Bromwich Albion in November 1962 for £15,000. He returned to Glasgow to play with Third Lanark and find success in business. He was also a capable golfer, playing to a two handicap.

Games:	154
Goals:	121
League Championship:	1956–57, 58–59
Born:	Falkirk

SAMMY BAIRD
1955–61

A graduate of the famous junior football academy Rutherglen Glencairn, Sammy Baird, a powerful left-side player, became a senior professional with Clyde. He moved to Preston North End in June 1954 when Scot Symon, then Preston manager, paid £12,000 for him. When Symon returned to Ibrox as manager he quickly bought Baird once more, in June of 1955 for £10,000. At 5' 11" and 12 st 8 lb, Baird used his physique to good effect, often being a very intimidating player. It was quite unwise to foul him. His upright running style earned him the tag 'Straight backed S.B.' and this, plus his blond hair, made it difficult to ignore him on the field. Baird was very much a type of inside-forward long identified with Rangers – big, industrious, strong in finishing. Prior to the 1990 World Cup final competition, Sammy was the only Rangers player to have scored in the World Cup finals.

Games:	179
Goals:	52
League Championship:	1955–56, 56–57
Scottish Cup:	1959–60
Honours:	7 Scotland caps
Born:	Denny, 13 May 1930

NORMAN ARNISON
1955–57

A South African centre-forward who joined the club in August 1955. Brother of Billy.

Games:	2
Goals:	2
Born:	Johannesburg

JIMMY MILLAR
1955–67

Above all else a dashing centre-forward as courageous as any player Rangers have ever had, Jimmy Millar was brave, honest, a never-say-die player who gave the impression that he would in fact die for the cause if there were no alternative. But Jimmy was not just a charging warhorse. He had skills and talent for the game in abundance, led his forward line well, was always in control of himself, and knew exactly what he was doing and trying to do. Although only 5' 6" tall, he was quite marvellous in the air and would knock balls down to Ralph Brand, who 'fed off' Jimmy for years, and with him formed a fearsome strike force. The 'M and B Tablets' they were dubbed in one of the greatest of Rangers teams, that of the early sixties which had Shearer, Caldow, Greig, McKinnon in defence, McMillan and Baxter in midfield, and Scott, Henderson and Wilson variously on the wings.

Millar was an outstanding half-back for Dunfermline when Rangers signed him for £5000 on 12 January 1955, and at times he played half-back at Ibrox. Fearless, gifted in ball control, Millar was a positive personality of much character who could be inspirational to team-mates. In May 1959, Millar was moved up to centre-forward in a match in Denmark when Max Murray was injured. The half-time score was 0–0. Rangers won 4–0 – Millar scored all four, and never looked back! Still he did win a Scottish Cup winners medal in 1966, as a wing -half towards the end of his Ibrox career. His international career was much compromised by injury. He went to Dundee United in the summer of 1967, was briefly manager of Raith Rovers, then took a pub in his native Edinburgh.

Games:	317
Goals:	160
League Championship:	1960–61, 62–63, 63–64
Scottish Cup:	1959–60, 61–62, 62–63, 63–64, 65–66
League Cup:	1960–61, 61–62, 64–65.
Honours:	2 Scotland caps
Born:	Edinburgh, 20 November 1934

RALPH BRAND
1954–65

Ralph Laidlaw Brand was seen by the Rangers manager, Bill Struth, on television when he played in the England *v* Scotland schoolboy international at Wembley in 1952. In June of that year the boy Brand was provisionally signed for Rangers, and in April 1954 he became a fully fledged Ranger, six months short of his eighteenth birthday. Indeed, he had made his debut before that on 6 November 1954. Willie Waddell and Willie McCulloch were both injured, and the young Brand played at outside-right. The match was against Kilmarnock – Rangers won 6–0 and Ralph Brand scored twice. It was an omen of things to come. Brand became one of the truly great Rangers goal-scorers.

He spent most of 1955 and 1956 doing National Service and by December 1957 was back in a Rangers team rather demoralised by a 7–1 defeat from Celtic in the League Cup Final of that year. He made twenty-two league appearances that season, scoring eleven goals. By season 1960–61 his partnership with Jimmy Millar was established and was to be the sharp end of a very successful Rangers team over the next half-dozen years. They first impressed as a partnership in the opening League Cup fixture of 1959–60, in an away match against Hibs which Rangers won 6–1 – four goals to Brand, one to Millar and one to Andy Matthew.

Brand was a player of intense concentration and constant movement. He put so much into a match that he'd often be sitting in the dressing room an hour after the match, still anxious to talk about it. He was a deep thinker on the game, wanting to talk tactics at a time when such discussion was probably in short supply at Ibrox. He was beautifully balanced on either side, as sharp and fearless as a Law or a Greaves in the penalty area, on the ground or in the air. At 5' 7" Ralph was no giant. He never weighed more than 150 lb, but speed off the mark was the thing for him, and above all a burning desire to be a great player. Even in primary school in Murrayburn in Edinburgh, he wanted to be a footballer. In seven Rangers finals, he was never on the losing side and scored six goals. In eight international matches, he scored eight goals! He was perhaps unfortunate in that Denis Law was a contemporary.

Brand always wanted to do extra-skills training. He wore lightweight continental boots when others were rejecting them. Oddly, he was never over-popular with the Ibrox crowd, who dismissed him as a poacher. Some poacher !

No doubt for the money and perhaps a new tactical stimulus, and with an outstanding Rangers team breaking up, he moved to Manchester City in August 1965 for a £30,000 fee, and two years later to Sunderland. He became a qualified FA coach and moved back to Raith Rovers in 1969, before retiring as a player in 1970.

Games:	317
Goals:	206
League Championship:	1958–59, 60–61, 62–63, 63–64
Scottish Cup:	1961–62, 62–63, 63–64
League Cup:	1960–61, 61–62, 63–64, 64–65
Honours:	8 Scotland caps
Born:	Edinburgh, 8 December 1936

DON KITCHENBRAND
1955–58

Don Kitchenbrand was signed from the South African club Delfos on 26 September 1955, and the appearance of the South African immediately split the Ibrox supporters into two camps, for and against. Kitchenbrand was hugely strong and fast, was nicknamed 'The Rhino', and quite simply knocked defenders down with his bulk as much as anything else. He was neither smart enough nor skilful enough to be a 'dirty' player, but he would simply chase everything in sight, catching right on the line balls which everyone else would have written off. He could score goals – in season 1955–56, twenty-three League goals in twenty-five matches. And on 8 March of that season he hit four out of the eight Rangers scored against Queen of the South, in the very first Scottish League match to be played by floodlight. Don was transferred to Sunderland on 5 March 1958, and later returned to South Africa.

Games: 37
Goals: 30
League Championship: 1955–56
Honours: 1 South Africa cap (against Scotland!)
Born: Johannesburg

BOBBY SHEARER
1955–65

A red-haired firebrand of a right-back, Bobby Shearer, or 'Captain Cutlass' as he was known, was a death-or-glory, take-no-prisoners defender for whom becoming captain of Rangers, as in time he did, was – the ultimate. Shearer was – is – the ultimate 'Blue-nose' and to this day will not tolerate a word of criticism of the club, no matter how well merited it might be. He was signed from Hamilton Academicals where his father was head groundsman, and for the best part of a decade was a good, if unpolished full-back who tackled with all the fierce intensity of a Jock Shaw. He formed a valuable full-back partnership with Eric Caldow in domestic football. His lack of pace would perhaps have left him exposed at higher levels of the game, in European and international competition, although he did play for Scotland four times. Few Rangers players have collected more trophies than Shearer. He once enjoyed a run of 165 consecutive games.

Games:	407
Goals:	4
League Championship:	1956–57, 58–59, 60–61, 62–63, 63–64
Scottish Cup:	1961–62, 62–63, 63–64
League Cup:	1960–61, 61–62, 63–64, 64–65
Honours:	4 Scotland caps
Born:	Hamilton, 29 December 1931

BILLY RITCHIE
1955–67

Billy Ritchie from Newtongrange was signed from Bathgate Thistle on 12 August 1954 and overlapped and eventually succeeded George Niven as the goalkeeper in one of the greatest of all Rangers teams, that of the early sixties.

He played his first match on 5 May, in a Charity Cup-tie at home to Third Lanark and secured a regular place in the second half of season 1957–58. National Service took him to Cyprus for all of the following season, and when he returned, George Niven's form was just too good. By 1961 he was in the team, and for the next five years was an outstanding goalkeeper in an outstanding Rangers team. Ritchie was undemonstrative and was considered the 'quiet man' of the team, but he was a solidly reliable goalkeeper who had a shutout in every third game he played for Rangers.

He had one cap for Scotland when he came on as a substitute for Eddie Connachan of Dunfermline in Scotland's match against Uruguay at Hampden. Ritchie's first handling of the ball was to pick it out of his net! He was probably unlucky on the international scene in being a contemporary of Bill Brown, the Dundee and Tottenham goalkeeper who won twenty-eight Scotland caps. Billy Ritchie's last game for Rangers was against Aberdeen in a League Cup semi-final at Hampden, drawn 2–2, on 19 October 1966. A year later, like George Niven before him, Billy Ritchie was transferred to Partick Thistle.

Games:	340
Shutouts:	120
League Championship:	1962–63, 63–64
Scottish Cup:	1961–62, 62–63, 63–64, 65–66
League Cup:	1961–62, 63–64, 64–65
Honours:	1 Scotland cap
Born:	Newtongrange, 11 September 1936

ALAN ELLIOT
1955–56

Alan was a centre-half, very fit, particularly hardy. The need for a replacement for George Young was becoming imminent and Alan might have been considered, but at 5' 9" he was probably not quite commanding enough. One of his only two games this season in place of Young was against Celtic at Parkhead, which Rangers won 1–0! He was given a free transfer at the end of the season.

Games: 2
Goals: 0
Born: Glasgow

SANDY THOMSON
1955–56

Centre-half who played in place of George Young in the opening League game of the season, but like Alan Elliot failed to escape from the reserve team. That match, at home to Stirling Albion, was a 0–0 draw.

Games: 1
Goals: 0
Born: Kilsyth

JOHN QUEEN
1955–58

An outstanding junior from the same team as Torry Gillick, Petershill Juniors, John was considered a potential successor to the great Rangers inside-right. Queen was a very skilful inside-forward with a near-mastery of the ball, but could not overcome the presence of Simpson, Baird and Murray and remained a reserve player.

Games: 2
Goals: 0
Born: Glasgow

WILLIE LOGIE
1956–57

From Cambuslang Rangers, big and strong, Logie looked as good a left-half as Rangers had had in years, but in their first venture in the European Champions Cup, in a rough-house match in Nice, he was ordered off with the French centre-forward Bravo, and his career seemed to go downhill from there.

Games: 19
Goals: 0
Born: Montreal

HAROLD DAVIS
1956–64

Very strong, very hard, very popular, right-half Davis, with Shearer and Greig and even Jimmy Millar, gave the outstanding Rangers team of the early sixties its bite, just as Baxter, McMillan, Brand and the wingers gave it style, skill, class and polish. Harold was signed from East Fife on 31 October 1956 by Scot Symon, who had kept a close watch on him, and like Symon himself, Davis was an excellent ball-winner and a much better footballer than many people thought. Although he looked slightly sluggish in action, he never seemed to be caught short of pace or out of position. He was particularly protective of Ian McMillan. Harold was a veteran of the Korean War, in which he was wounded. He remained a perfect gentleman, and became a very successful hotelier in Wester Ross.

Games:	261
Goals:	13
League Championship:	1956–57, 58–59, 60–61, 62–63
Scottish Cup:	1961–62
League Cup:	1960–61, 61–62
Born:	Cupar

DAVIE WILSON
1956–67

Arguably Rangers' finest outside-left since Alan Morton, Wilson, only 5' 6" tall and very fair haired, was fast, direct, opportunistic, with a particular talent for penalty-area positioning when the crosses from the outside-rights, Scott and Henderson, were pouring in. He had an outstanding career with Rangers and Scotland, one of his most famous internationals being against England at Wembley in 1963 when he moved to left-back and played with great distinction after Eric Caldow had broken a leg. One of his many important international goals was Scotland's first in the 2–0 win over England at Hampden in 1962. In March of that year he had scored six goals in Rangers' 7–1 win at Falkirk.

Wilson, a Glasgow boy, was signed from Baillieston Juniors in May of 1956. In August 1967, at the age of twenty-eight, he and Wilson Wood went to Dundee United in exchange for Orjan Persson, and he had five good seasons there. Many people felt that Rangers had released him too soon. He went to Dumbarton in 1972 where he became assistant manager, and later, successfully, manager.

Games:	373
Goals:	155
League Championship:	1960–61, 62–63
Scottish Cup:	1959–60, 61–62, 62–63, 63–64, 65–66
League Cup:	1960–61, 61–62
Honours:	22 Scotland caps
Born:	Glasgow, 10 January 1939

BILLY SMITH
1956–58

A centre-half or full-back who joined the club in June 1955, from Dundee North End, Billy was from Arbroath, where his family owned fishing boats. At 5' 9", and perhaps on the slow side, Billy never did break through with Rangers and played a total of only three first-team games, one of them a Glasgow Charity Cup tie in May 1958. He was released a year later.

Games: 2
Goals: 2
Born: Arbroath

BOBBY MORRISON
1956–58

Bobby Morrison was a tall, slim inside-left who had looked a really good player at Falkirk, where he came from, but he didn't register at Ibrox and was freed on 1 May 1958.

Games: 8
Goals: 7
Born: Chapelhall

JOHN VALENTINE
1956–57

John was signed from Queen's Park on 2 May 1956, and Rangers thought they had a fine centre-half in the making. But John was unfortunate. He played in the League Cup Final on 19 October 1957, when Celtic won 7–1 and completely outclassed and even humiliated Rangers. Billy McPhail, the Celtic centre-forward against Valentine, scored three goals. Within a month, perhaps paranoid about that result, Rangers had signed the experienced Willie Telfer from St Mirren for £10,000. Valentine never again played for the first team and a year later was transferred to St Johnstone.

Games: 9
Goals: 0
Born: Buckie

ALAN AUSTIN
1957–58

Austin was pitched into the early-season Celtic match at Ibrox, playing left-half in a game in which Rangers were by no means favourites. Some supporters saw this as a scapegoat selection. Rangers lost 3–2. The left-half position had been troubling Rangers at this time, and they used variously Davis, Millar and Baird.

Games: 1
Goals: 0
Born: Glasgow

WILLIE TELFER
1957–60

Telfer, already an experienced and international player and thirty-two years of age, was signed in November 1957 as a stop-gap following the defeat, humiliating for Rangers, of 7–1 by Celtic in the final of the League Cup a month earlier. If the £10,000 signing from St Mirren was a knee-jerk reaction by the Ibrox club, it was a resounding success and one of their most profitable purchases. Powerfully built, Telfer was a bustling, vigorous, rational centre-half of experience who held Rangers together and allowed the club to assemble their outstanding team of the early sixties. In spite of his physique, he was a gentleman and a player of honesty with a respect for the game. On one famous occasion in a Scotland–Wales match at Hampden which was Telfer's one international appearance, John Charles, the magnificent Wales centre-forward, got past Telfer and made for goal. Telfer, half a yard behind him, could easily have brought Charles down with a 'professional foul', but chose not to. Charles went on and scored. Telfer was much criticised, and was never again selected for Scotland. The match was drawn 3–3.

Games:	97
Goals:	0
League Championship:	1958–59
Honours:	1 Scotland cap
Born:	Larkhall, 26 October 1925

WILLIE MOLES
1957–58

Moles was a centre-half who to some extent replaced John Valentine following that League Cup Final defeat by Celtic, but held the place only until Willie Telfer had arrived and settled into the position after a few weeks. The sequence of Valentine – Moles–Telfer was the result of the quest by Rangers to find a worthwhile successor to George Young following the Woodburn suspension.

Games:	5
Goals:	0
Born:	Airdrie

GEORGE DUNCAN
1957–60

An outside-right, a little fellow who was a perfectly good player but who had bleak prospects with Alex Scott at the club.

Games:	15
Goals:	5
Born:	Glasgow

BILLY HOGG
1957–59

Centre-forward or inside-forward who was signed from
Aberdeen on a free transfer.

Games: 2
Goals: 1
Born: Glasgow

TOM ROBERTSON
1957–58

An inside-forward from Edinburgh – a very skilful player in
short, sharp bursts. His only game was a League Cup semi-
final against Brechin City, won 4–0 by Rangers. He was
freed on 1 May 1958.

Games: 1
Goals: 0
Born: Kincardine

ANDY McEWAN
1958–59

A centre-forward from Queen's Park, Andy arrived in June
1958 and was freed in April 1959.

Games: 1
Goals: 0
Born: Glasgow

HARRY MELROSE
1957–58

An elegant, skilful little player from the Edinburgh area,
Harry was freed on 1 May 1958 and went to Dunfermline
Athletic where he had a perfectly good career, winning a
Scottish Cup winner's medal in 1961 against Celtic. His one
game for Rangers was that League Cup semi-final in which
Robertson played. Harry had two of the four goals.

Games: 1
Goals: 2
Born: Edinburgh

Dunfermline Athletic
Scottish Cup: 1960–61

BILL PATERSON
1958–62

Bill Paterson, a former Scotland 'B' international player, was signed in July 1958 from Newcastle United for £3500. He became the bridging centre-half between Willie Telfer and Ronnie McKinnon, the latter playing through most of the sixties. Paterson was tall and stylish, good-looking and in the opinion of some of Rangers' fundamentalist fans, too gentlemanly and not physical enough to be the ideal Rangers centre-half. Without ever looking like a full international player, Bill played well, and stabilised the position for the club. He was a close friend of fellow half-back Harold Davis – they often went fishing together. Bill was given a free transfer on 21 September 1962.

Games:	116
Goals:	0
League Championship:	1960–61
Scottish Cup:	1959–60
League Cup:	1960–61
Born:	Kinlochleven

BOBBY ORR
1958–59

Big, strong, direct right-half. Freed in April 1960, and became a policeman.

Games:	1
Goals:	0
Born:	Bellshill

ANDY MATTHEW
1958–60

Andy Matthew was signed from East Fife on 17 July 1958 for a fee of £4500, and he gave Rangers reasonable service. He was a fast, direct, orthodox outside-left with a natural left foot, and if not the bravest of wingers, he would nevertheless persist in getting to the byeline and getting his crosses in, thus doing exactly what his manager, Scot Symon, felt a winger should do. He was particularly successful in European matches. Rangers got their money back when he returned to Fife, and Raith Rovers, on 11 September 1960 for exactly £4500.

Games:	37
Goals:	12
League Championship:	1958–59
Born:	Kirkcaldy

BILLY STEVENSON
1958–62

A red-haired left-half, an excellent footballer in a good Rangers team, Billy seemed put out by the expensive arrival of Jim Baxter in June 1960, for his position, in a transfer that was to mean the completion of one of the greatest Rangers teams. In the pre-Baxter season of 1959–60 Stevenson had played thirty-four League games, indeed had been Rangers' only ever-present in all matches. In Baxter's first season, 1960–61, he played only eight games, and in the next season only five. Billy didn't care for this, and he swept off to Australia at the end of that season. He was back in the autumn, and was transferred to Liverpool for £20,000 on 19 October 1962 and had an excellent career at Anfield under Bill Shankly. Stevenson completed a Scotland–England Cup double in 1965, as his former Rangers compadre Alex Scott was to do with Everton a year later.

Games:	103
Goals:	1
League Championship:	1958–59
Scottish Cup:	1959–60
Born:	Leith
Liverpool	
FA Cup:	1964–65
Football League Championship:	1963–64, 1965–66

IAN McMILLAN
1958–64

Ian McMillan, dubbed the 'Wee Prime Minister' because of his control of affairs and in recognition of the then Prime Minister Harold McMillan, was an old-style inside-forward and a player of the highest class. He was arguably the most gifted inside-right Rangers have had since Torry Gillick. Adept at screening the ball from defenders, his technical skills gave him instant and total control of the ball. He was an exceptional strategist, and this with his ball control allowed him to dictate the pace and tempo of a game and in particular set up open, running chances with through-balls to the forceful strikers, Jimmy Millar and Ralph Brand. He was at Ibrox for only six years, but it was a period which brought as much concentrated success to the club as did any in its history.

When he joined Rangers on 2 October 1958 he was twenty-seven years old and had a decade of senior football with Airdrieonians under his studs, and was already an international player. His first match was against Raith Rovers at Ibrox, producing the result of 4–4, with McMillan scoring the first and last Rangers goal. Rangers had been having a spell of rather indifferent form, but from that match on, with the arrival of McMillan, they went twenty-three matches with only one defeat; Ian played a season's total of twenty-six matches, scoring nine goals, and Rangers won the Championship by two points from Hearts! If ever a player gave a team the kiss of life, it was McMillan for Rangers in 1958–59.

With the advent of Jim Baxter in the summer of 1960, one of the great Rangers inside-forward partnerships was in place. They would be called midfield players today, but neither McMillan nor Baxter was much for defending or tackling, and neither was much inclined to head the ball. But McMillan was sustained – to some extent protected – by his right-half Harold Davis, a hardy, hard-tackling, ball-winning Fifer, and Baxter by the defensive talents of such as Greig and McKinnon, and with the speed of Caldow behind him.

These two players, McMillan and Baxter, were the controllers, the architects, the engineers of Rangers in the first half of the sixties. Neither was addicted to running – they made the ball run for them. McMillan relied on his skills; he was not a physical player but he was a good, talented, old-fashioned dribbler who knew how to work with a winger. He formed exceptional right-wing partnerships with first Alex Scott, then with Willie Henderson, during his time at Ibrox. His work might well have been rewarded with more Scottish international honours than he enjoyed.

He played his last game for Rangers on 29 April 1964 against St Johnstone at Perth, a match which Rangers lost 1–0 to finish a season in which they won the Championship from Kilmarnock by six points, a 'Triple Crown' season. McMillan, a qualified quantity surveyor, had always been a part-time player at Ibrox. In December of that year he went back to Airdrie, retired from playing in the close season of 1967 after the best part of twenty years as a player, then became coach, manager and subsequently a director of his home-town club, no doubt his first and last love. But in between, there had been golden, light-blue days.

Games:	194
Goals:	55
League Championship:	1958–59, 60–61
Scottish Cup:	1959–60, 61–62, 62–63
League Cup:	1960–61, 61–62
Honours:	6 Scotland caps, (1 with Rangers)
Born:	Airdrie, 18 March 1931

DAVID PROVAN
1958–70

David, a Falkirk boy standing 6' 2", came from Bonnyvale Star as a centre-half but was kept out of that slot by Paterson and McKinnon. Nicely balanced, he could play either full-back position, and his chance came when Eric Caldow suffered a broken leg in the Wembley international of 1963. He matured from being a solid club craftsman to international class in the mid sixties, and in his long career at Ibrox was in full-back partnerships with Caldow, Bobby Shearer and Kai Johansen. He played in the European Cup Winners' Cup Final of 1967. Released by Willie Waddell in 1970, he played with Crystal Palace, Plymouth Argyle and St Mirren, retiring in the summer of 1975. He was assistant manager to Alex Ferguson at St Mirren, manager of Albion Rovers for a spell, and chief scout for Rangers under John Greig's management.

Games:	262
Goals:	11
League Championship:	1963–64
Scottish Cup:	1962–63, 63–64, 65–66
League Cup:	1963–64, 64–65
Honours:	5 Scotland caps
Born:	Falkirk, 11 March 1941

NORRIE MARTIN
1958–70

Norrie Martin came to Ibrox as third-choice goalkeeper to George Niven and Billy Ritchie, and succeeded in becoming surely the unluckiest footballer who ever played for Rangers. He played his first match, an important League Cup tie against Hearts at Tynecastle on 23 August 1958, and played quite brilliantly until he was carried off with what proved to be a fractured skull. It was to be more than two years before he played in the first team again. Almost seven years later to the day – 21 August 1965 *versus* Aberdeen at Pittodrie when he was pressing to make the position his own – it happened again. He was carried off with a fractured skull. By 1966–67 he was number one with thirty-eight matches, but fate was not finished with Norrie Martin. He was in goal on 28 January 1967 when Berwick Rangers beat Glasgow Rangers 1–0 in the most sensational result in the history of Rangers, perhaps of the Scottish Cup competition. As Scot Symon said, 'This is the worst result in the club's history.'

That season Rangers were runners-up in League, League Cup and European Cup Winners' Cup. The following season Norrie lost his place to Eric Sorensen from Morton, then won it back again only to lose it to the German Gerry Neef. He played for the last time on 11 October 1969, against Hibs at Ibrox, when the visitors uncharitably won 3–1, and in April of 1970 he was given a free transfer by manager Willie Waddell.

Norrie Martin left with just a clutch of reserve-team honours and several runners-up medals, surely unprecedented for anyone who had spent twelve years with Rangers.

Games:	109
Shutouts:	41
Born:	Ladybank

GEORGE McLEAN (2)
1962–67

Signed for a then-record fee between Scottish clubs of £26,500 from St Mirren in January 1963, George Tomlinson 'Dandy' McLean was one of the most enigmatic and controversial figures to play for Rangers since 1945. Originally a wing-half, he forced himself on the attention of Rangers when he played very well against them for St Mirren in the 1962 Scottish Cup Final, which Rangers won 2–0. He could play equally well at inside-forward, and the Rangers thinking was that he might succeed Ian McMillan, although he was a quite different type of player. At 6' 1" and none too physical, he could appear almost cumbersome on the ball at times but his distribution was cultured and constructive, and when he was played as a striker by manager Scot Symon he scored netfuls of goals by the side of Jim Forrest.

George was indeed 'Dandy' – a sharp dresser, a driver of quality cars, a lad for the good life off the field. Scot Symon had some problems in trying to control him, but there was nothing malicious in it all. He was quick with the repartee, a match for Jim Baxter at any time.

He scored ten minutes from the end of the Scottish Cup semi-final of 1966 against Aberdeen to put Rangers in the final, missed the final, then played in the final replay in place of Jim Forrest, against Celtic. Rangers won 1–0, and in all matches that season of 1965–66 George scored no fewer than forty-one goals. His last match for the club came the following January when he and Forrest were held to be the villains, the guilty men responsible for the infamous Rangers Scottish Cup defeat at Berwick. Rangers were certainly paranoid about it. In March, Forrest went to Preston North End for £38,000 and in April, George McLean went to Dundee in exchange for Andy Penman. He later played for Dunfermline Athletic, Ayr United and Hamilton Accies.

Games:	116
Goals:	82
League Championship:	1963–64
Scottish Cup:	1963–64, 65–66
Honours:	1 Scotland cap
Born:	Paisley, 26 May 1943

GEORGE McLEAN (1)
1959–62

George was the first of two George McLeans, which can be confusing to Rangers archivists. He was a centre- or inside-forward who found the competition too stiff, and he was transferred to Norwich City on 22 March 1962.

Games:	8
Goals:	3
Born:	Paisley

BOBBY HUME
1959–62

A rather small, lightweight outside-left, Bobby was at the club in the reign of Davie Wilson, but in his few matches he never let Rangers down. He played in the first leg of the 1961 European Cup Winners' Cup Final at Ibrox, which Rangers lost 2–0 to Fiorentina. A forward line that read Wilson, McMillan, Scott, Brand and Hume was not a success. On 14 September 1962 Bobby Hume transferred to Middlesbrough for £10,000. He later went to play and live in South Africa. He was rather short-sighted, which probably affected his play.

Games:	23
Goals:	3
Born:	Glasgow

ALBERT FRANKS
1959–60

Albert Franks, an Englishman, was signed by Scot Symon from Newcastle United on 23 March 1960. He was never able to establish himself, although the intention was that he should succeed Harold Davis at wing-half. He had been a policeman before becoming a footballer, and he went back to a police career.

Games:	3
Goals:	0
Born:	Boldon, County Durham

STAN ANDERSON
1959–60

A Hamilton boy, Stan had a short spell at Ibrox as a left-side midfield player before moving on to Queen of the South. He was a coach at Ibrox in the seventies for Willie Waddell, then for Jock Wallace, and was manager of Clyde for a time.

Games: 1
Goals: 0
Born: Craigneuk

BOBBY GRANT
1959–60

A centre-forward, Bobby came directly from Edinburgh juvenile football in July 1959.

Games: 1
Goals: 0
Born: Edinburgh

WILLIE PENMAN
1960–63

Willie, a Fifer, was a fine junior footballer and was in the St Andrews United team which won the final of the Scottish Junior Cup. He played inside-left, understudy to Ralph Brand, but was transferred to Newcastle United on 4 April 1963 for £11,500 in 1960. He was substitute for Swindon Town when the Third Division team beat Arsenal 3–1 in the English League Cup Final of 1969, on a Wembley mudheap.

Games: 3
Goals: 0
Born: Coaltown of Wemyss

DOUG BAILLIE
1960–64

Douglas Baillie was a first-team centre-half at the age of seventeen in an Airdrie team that included Tony Harris, Ian McMillan and goalkeeper Jock Wallace. He had been a schoolboy international player and was quite outstanding as a youth. He was tall at 6'2", huge and immensely powerful and could be instantly intimidating by virtue of his bulk. Scot Symon saw this giant as a colossus around whom future Rangers teams could be built, and in the summer of 1960 paid Airdrie £18,000 for him. Baillie was difficult to beat in the air and difficult to pass on the ground; there was so much of him. He was used occasionally as a centre-forward to upset and frighten defences, one such occasion being the Ibrox semi-final of the European Cup Winners' Cup in 1961 against Wolves, which Rangers won 2-0. Roger Hynd, in the final of the same competition six years later, played the same role with the same limited success. Douglas always had a weight problem. In September 1964 he was exchanged for Findlay McGillivray of Third Lanark, who never did play in the Rangers first team. Baillie also played for Dunfermline and Falkirk before becoming chief football writer at the *Sunday Post*, succeeding the famous Jack Harkness.

Games: 40
Goals: 0
League Cup: 1961–62
Born: Douglas, 27 January 1937

JIM BAXTER
1960–65, 1969–70

Just as many good and sober judges would claim John Greig to be the greatest Rangers player of all, a claim needless to say that is beyond any proof, so they might well insist that Jim Baxter was the most extravagantly gifted of all Rangers players. Many critics declared that he was the best left-sided player Rangers had seen since the fabled Alan Morton. Willie Waddell said boldly that he was 'the most skilful left-half ever produced by Rangers'. At all events, it would not be too prejudiced a claim to say that he was a keystone of one of the best of all Rangers teams, that of 1960–65.

He was superbly gifted – his ball skills were astonishing, especially with his left foot. His defensive qualities were not worth speaking of, however, and he was very fortunate to have a full-back of the pace and resolution of Eric Caldow behind him. It was said that 'Slim Jim' could not tackle, could not use his right foot, could not head the ball. (Jimmy Greaves 'couldn't' tackle, Puskas of Hungary 'couldn't' use his right foot, Stanley Matthews 'couldn't' head the ball!) Baxter was an individualist, his own man. Work rate did not loom high in his priorities – so much so that, had he been English, he might not have been considered for a place in Alf Ramsey's England team of the time. Baxter had to be the dominant personality, the orchestrator of the ensemble, the king of the castle. The bigger the stage, the better.

He was certainly a player for the big occasion. He loved the 'Old Firm' matches, loved 'taking the mickey' out of Celtic when he could. One of the most vivid examples of this was the replay of the 1963 Scottish Cup Final, when Rangers demoralised Celtic with a 3–0 win. Indeed, Baxter had a remarkable record in these matches. In the period 1960–65 he played eighteen times for Rangers against Celtic, ten League matches, five in the League Cup and three in the Scottish Cup, and was only twice on the losing side. What gave Baxter even more impish pleasure was in doing the same thing against England at Wembley in the matches of 1963, when he scored both goals in a 2–1 win, and again in 1967 in a 3–2 win. His career was marked by both brilliance and self-indulgence. Although Scottish fans, always neurotically obsessed with the ball-player above all else, worshipped these performances and maintain their memory in the lore of the game, they were no more than parades of the Baxter trait of an unlimited confidence which bordered on arrogance. Nevertheless, he was a player of the highest class. In October 1963, in England's centenary match against the Rest of the World, he was in the World squad of players and took part in the match in place of Masopust of Czechoslovakia.

Rangers paid a record Scottish fee of £17,500 when they signed him from Raith Rovers on 21 June 1960. A Fifer, he had been a part-time player with Raith, encouraged and directed to an extent by Willie McNaught, the team's Scottish international left-back. For a spell, Baxter had worked in coal mining. He was one of the last young men required to do National Service, which he did in the Black Watch. He established himself immediately in a Rangers team which manager Scot Symon had assembled and which was to dominate the Scottish game for five years. Baxter's languid left-sided attacking play combined perfectly with Ian McMillan's generalship on the right. But Baxter's was a wayward genius. He never seemed prepared to pay the price of discipline and dedication which great talent demands if it is to thrive and mature. Symon would say to him 'You're the man who makes Rangers play. Go out and make them play.' He eventually captained the team, and it may be that such responsibilities were not for Jim. He did not much care for training; he never saw much merit in work for its own sake. He also drank quite heavily, as he himself has admitted.

Baxter's time at Ibrox was punctuated by several signing and wages squabbles and he was transferred to Sunderland in May 1965 for £72,500. He moved to Nottingham Forest in December of 1967 for £100,000 and no doubt his share of the fees was reason enough for these moves. By this time, Baxter's off-the-field activities had more media attention than his play. He returned to Rangers in May 1969, unsuccessfully, and retired in November of the following year to become a publican.

Games:	254
Goals:	24
League Championship:	1960–61, 62–63, 63–64
Scottish Cup:	1961–62, 62–63, 63–64
League Cup:	1960–61, 61–62, 63–64, 64–65
Honours:	34 Scotland caps (24 with Rangers)
Born:	Hill o' Beath, 29 September 1939

RON McKINNON
1960–73

Without much doubt, Ronnie McKinnon was the best centre-half Rangers had had since Willie Woodburn. He was a product of Benburb, the local Govan junior team, and of Dunipace Juniors, and he signed for Rangers in 1959 as a wing-half. However, he developed as a centre-half in the reserves. He was considered a stop-gap when coming into the team in 1961–62, with both Paterson and Baillie injured, but developed into an international class defender, and throughout most of the sixties shared the centre-half position in the Scotland team with Billy McNeill, the Celtic captain. At 5' 10¹/₂" he was not over-tall for a centre-half and in his early seasons he was criticised for being weak in the air. This was exploited by Spurs in a European Cup Winners' Cup match in 1962 when Rangers were beaten 5–2 at White Hart Lane.

But McKinnon worked hard at his game, and became a well-rounded footballer. He was composed, stylish, authoritative, and had a calming effect on the Rangers defence. He never seemed under much pressure in possession, and was entirely comfortable with the good players around him. The line of Greig–McKinnon–Baxter was one of the finest in the history of the club, and of Scotland, reaching a peak perhaps in the 3–2 win at Wembley in 1967. In the late sixties, in the face of Celtic's dominance, Greig and McKinnon were the heart of the Rangers defence, and carried the team on their shoulders. Ron broke a leg in the away European match against Sporting Lisbon in November 1971 and so missed a chance of playing in Rangers' European Cup Winners' Cup triumph in May 1972. He left Rangers at the end of season 1972–73, played for a year in South Africa, then moved on to Australia.

Games:	473
Goals:	3
League Championship:	1962–63, 63–64
Scottish Cup:	1961–62, 62–63, 63–64, 65–66
League Cup:	1963–64, 64–65, 70–71
Honours:	28 Scotland caps
Born:	Glasgow, 20 August 1940

WILLIE HENDERSON
1960–72

As popular with Ibrox fans as any player in modern times, Willie Henderson was at least the equal of any of the great wingers who have graced Rangers' long history. He was an outside-right of the most tremendous pace, muscled and closely coupled at 5' 4" like the sprinter he was. He could weave through a warren of defence, a maze of defenders, as he pleased, to the extreme delight of the fans. His speed, dribbling skills and ball control, his ability to change direction quickly on a dead run – dummying inside the full-back was a feature of his game – and the quality of his crossing to Millar and Brand, and even to Davie Wilson on the far side of the penalty area, made him one of Rangers' most highly profitable players.

Willie was something of a boy prodigy. He was a schoolboy international with Airdrie Schools, one of the few who made the transition to full international status. He was capped by Scotland at the age of 18 years 269 days. Only Denis Law in the modern era played for Scotland at a younger age, about one month earlier than Henderson. Willie was in the Rangers team at eighteen and stayed there, hastening the departure of Alex Scott to Everton. He had his share of injuries, and in season 1964–65 a bunion operation caused him several months of inaction. He was a direct contemporary of Jimmy Johnstone, the brilliant Celtic outside-right, and in the first half of the sixties was probably the more effective player. In the second half of the decade, Johnstone, playing in an exceptional Celtic team, probably had the edge. Between them, they dominated the position in the Scotland team throughout the decade.

Henderson had some eyesight difficulties, and wore contact lenses. The story is told – it deserves to be true – of how, late in an Old Firm match, he rushed over to the bench and asked, 'How long to go, how long to go?' Jock Stein replied, 'Go and ask at the other dugout, you bloody fool – this is the Celtic bench!'

Henderson moved to Sheffield Wednesday in July 1972 and in 1974 to the Rangers of Hong Kong, where he captained the national team. He finished his career, aptly, with Airdrie in 1979.

Games:	426
Goals:	62
League Championship:	1962–63, 63–64
Scottish Cup:	1961–62, 62–63, 63–64, 65–66
League Cup:	1963–64, 70–71
Honours:	29 Scotland caps
Born:	Baillieston, 24 January 1944

JOHN GREIG
1961–78

John Greig is considered by many good and sober judges to have been the greatest of all Rangers players. It is a subjective claim, of course, but there is a powerful body of opinion, and of fact, to support the claim. Greig made 857 appearances in all for the club, second only to the total of Dougie Gray, the full-back who played in the twenties, thirties and forties. But for becoming manager of the club in May 1978, when he was still an active player, he would have passed Gray's total. He played for Scotland forty-four times, twenty-one matches in succession, and captained his country. Three times in his career he was part of a treble-winning Rangers team – League, Scottish Cup and League Cup – in 1963–64, 75–76 and 77–78. Twice he played in a European final, the Cup Winners' Cup on each occasion – in 1967 when Rangers lost to Bayern Munich 1–0 after extra time, and in 1972 when they beat Moscow Dynamo 3–2 in Barcelona. In his sixteen seasons with Rangers he averaged close to one honour per season. Many a footballer has played an entire career that long without winning one. For his services to football, John Greig was awarded an MBE.

In many ways he epitomised the spirit of the club. Even in the most hopeless of lost causes, Greig would fight to the finish; he was indomitable. He was not the most skilful of players – the quality of his passing was variable, and many defenders have been more accurate in their use of the ball. But he was above all a leader of men, a great club servant and captain for whom the club was life and who carried the team for many years when Jock Stein's Celtic was sweeping all before it, in the second half of the sixties. He did it by being 'one of the boys' off the field, and by example, exhortation and leadership on it. When it was necessary, Greig could take the team by the scruff of the neck and shake it into shape.

He was often selected for Rangers teams in an inside-forward position (he had a powerful shot, and scored in his first match, against Airdrie at Ibrox in the League Cup in September 1961), but his natural position was as a central defender or sweeper, where he was a hard but never evil competitor. Indeed, in the outstanding Rangers teams of the early sixties which won three Championships in four years, the core of the defence was Greig and Ron McKinnon, in front of goalkeeper Billy Ritchie. They were the foundation on which Jim Baxter and Ian McMillan could build their attacking patterns, while players such as Jimmy Millar and Ralph Brand put away the goals. Greig, McKinnon and Baxter was the outstanding half-back line of the day.

From 1966 to 1970, Rangers won nothing. In the League Championship they had a long barren spell from 1964 to 1975, as the greatest of all Celtic teams dominated the Scottish game with nine successive Championships. When Baxter, McMillan, Brand, Millar, Shearer and Caldow had gone, Greig and McKinnon soldiered on, and although many supporters viewed the late sixties as a time of failure and crisis, the fact is that Rangers were a very good second to Celtic at a time when both were streets ahead of all other Scottish teams. And Rangers were at least relatively successful in Europe – finalists in the Cup Winners' Cup in 1961 and 1967, quarter-finalists in the Fairs Cities Cup of 1968, semi-finalists in 1969 and, at last, with John Greig as an inspiring captain, winners of the European Cup Winners' Cup in 1972. The team of the late sixties/early seventies was probably better than many a Rangers team that did win the Championship.

As a player, Greig will never be forgotten by Rangers fans for his resolution, his leadership, his dedication. For his 1978 testimonial match no fewer than a staggering 65,000 packed into Ibrox. After five years as manager of the club, John was active as a travel consultant and a broadcaster on the game. In January 1990 he returned to Ibrox as manager of public relations for the club.

Games:	753
Goals:	120
League Championship:	1962–63, 63–64, 74–75, 75–76, 77–78
Scottish Cup:	1962–63, 63–64, 65–66, 72–73, 75–76, 77–78
League Cup:	1963–64, 64–65, 75–76, 77–78
European Cup Winners' Cup:	1971–72
Honours:	44 Scotland caps
Born:	Edinburgh, 11 September 1942

JIM CHRISTIE
1961–62

Signed on 22 May 1961 for £11,000 from Ayr United, for whom he had played in only ten first-team games, Jim was a direct, capable player whose appearances were restricted by Jimmy Millar. Nevertheless, his scoring record was a centre-forward's dream and included some important goals, not least two in Rangers' 3–2 win over Monaco at Ibrox on 5 September in the European Champions Cup of 1961–62.

Games: 8
Goals: 8
Born: Glasgow

CRAIG WATSON
1962–66

A reserve to David Wilson, Craig was a lively outside-left with a lot of pace. He played several matches in 1963–64, when Wilson was injured, including a European Champions Cup tie second leg, when Rangers were overwhelmed by Real Madrid in Spain 6–0. He went to Morton in exchange for Jorn Sorensen in August 1965.

Games: 20
Goals: 4
League Cup   1963-64
Born: Glasgow

BOBBY KING
1961–62

A full-back, and very much a reserve-team player, Bobby came directly from junior football as a youngster and was cover for Shearer or Caldow. One important match he did play was the first leg of the quarter-final tie of the Champions Cup against Standard Liège in Belgium. Rangers lost 4–1 and went out at that stage.

Games: 3
Goals: 0
Born: Edinburgh

WILLIE HUNTER
1962–64

A left-side midfield player from Hamilton Schools, Willie finished playing when he left Ibrox, and settled in Canada.

Games: 1
Goals: 0
Born: Cambuslang

DEREK TRAILL
1963–66

A fringe player from Edinburgh, outside-left Derek found the competition from Rangers wingers in the sixties too much for him.

Games: 5
Goals: 0
Born: Edinburgh

ALEX REID
1964–68

An inside-right, Alex joined Rangers in April 1964, and was given a free transfer on 17 June 1968.

Games: 2
Goals: 2
Born: Glasgow

JIM FORREST
1962–67

A goal-scorer *par excellence*, indeed a goal-scorer extraordinary as his goals-to-games-played ratio testifies, Jim Forrest was the ideal centre-forward – balanced, good on either foot, with an electrifying burst of speed, fearless, forbidding in the air. In spite of being criticised (quite wrongly) for being nothing but a goal-scorer (!), Forrest could combine unselfishly with other players and hold an attacking line together very well. One of a handful of players since 1945 to score a hundred League goals, his tally of fifty–seven goals in all matches in 1964–65 remains a record to this day. Forrest displaced the highly popular Jimmy Millar and came in as the successful team of the early sixties was breaking up. His Ibrox career ended under the cloud of the infamous Scottish Cup defeat at Berwick in January 1967. He and George McLean (2) were deemed entirely to blame, which was a nonsense, and were dropped and transferred within a few weeks. The transfer of Forrest, a gentleman in every respect, was quickly seen to have been a major error on the part of a paranoid management.

He had come to Rangers as a schoolboy, then been sent briefly to Drumchapel Amateurs for development. After a year at Preston he returned to Aberdeen and won a Scottish Cup medal with the Dons of 1970. He went to Hong Kong Rangers in 1973. His cousin Alex Willoughby was a colleague at Drumchapel, Rangers, Aberdeen and Hong Kong, a remarkable instance of family loyalty (or affection, or coincidence, or whatever). When Forrest scored a record four goals in the League Cup Final of 1963 against Morton, Willoughby scored the other in Rangers' 5–0 win. Jim Forrest scored four goals more than once, and on 30 October 1965 scored five against Hamilton Accies at Douglas Park in a 7–1 Rangers win.

Games:	164
Goals:	145
League Championship:	1963–64
League Cup:	1963–64, 64–65
Honours:	5 Scotland caps (2 with Rangers)
Born:	Glasgow, 22 September 1944
Aberdeen	
Scottish Cup:	1969–70

ALEC WILLOUGHBY
1962–69

Inside-forward Alec joined Rangers at the same time as his cousin, Jim Forrest. They had both served a preliminary apprenticeship with Drumchapel Amateurs. Alec was a highly talented player who moved around in the stealthy fashion of the late John White in the famous Tottenham 'double' team of the sixties. Ironically, his real chance came after Rangers' infamous defeat at Berwick in January 1967, for which cousin Jim was condemned, and Willoughby was converted from a stylish midfield player into a striker and successful goal-scorer.

His achievements saw a sequence after the Berwick match as follows: 4 February *v* Hearts, three goals; 8 February *v* Clyde, three goals; 11 February *v* Kilmarnock, one goal; 1 March *v* Real Zaragossa, one goal; 4 March *v* Motherwell, four goals – a total of twelve goals in five games. In the following eight matches, Willoughby scored four of the team's total of thirteen. He was an outgoing personality, friendly, popular with everyone, in particular the Rangers crowd – an early-day Alistair McCoist – and a keen student of the game. He was inexplicably dropped in favour of Roger Hynd for the second-leg match at Ibrox in the European Cup Winners' Cup against Slavia Sofia, and again for the final against Bayern Munich in Nuremburg, as well as for decisive League matches late in the season, these omissions surely leading indirectly to the loss of the Championship and the European trophy.

In hindsight, Willoughby's treatment was seen as a major error of judgement on the part of Scot Symon, and although Alec was an out-and-out Rangers fan, he asked for a transfer. However, with the advent of Davie White as the new manager he became more of a regular for the next two seasons. The arrival of Andy Penman limited his appearances and he was transferred on 31 May 1969 to Aberdeen for £25,000, later playing in Hong Kong. When his playing career was over he became manager of Rangers Supporters Social Club, near the Ibrox ground. With Eric Caldow, he is now hosting the new executive facilities at Ibrox.

Games:	93
Goals:	47
League Cup	1963–64
Born:	Glasgow

ROGER HYND
1963–69

Roger, nephew of Bill and Bob Shankly (his mother was a Shankly), came out of Lanark Grammar School, big, strong, solid, an all-action, play-anywhere defender. He was whole-hearted, but alas never a player of the highest quality – by his own admission 'of limited ability'. Roger was a good squad player for the club, covering a number of defensive positions as required. His misfortune was that Scot Symon, on the basis of one, and only one, reserve game in which Hynd, playing centre-forward in an emergency, scored four goals in a 5-2 win, decided that he was ideally suited for the position. Four days later Hynd found himself playing centre-forward in a European Cup Winners' Cup semi-final against Slavia Sofia. At that level his shortcomings were savagely exposed, and he was simply miscast. Nevertheless, he was selected for the final of 1967 against Bayern Munich in Nuremberg, where he was consumed by a young central defender, name of Franz Beckenbauer. With half an hour gone in this match, Hynd, from the six-yard line, missed the only decent chance Rangers had in the match and with the score then 0–0, one which might well have won them the match. Roger was completely committed to Rangers and in a fit of pique and disgust at the end of the match, he threw his medal into the Nuremberg crowd. Only then did he learn that winners' and losers' medals were identical. But his was gone forever.

On 22 June 1969 he joined Crystal Palace for £25,000, later played for Birmingham City, and managed Motherwell for a spell. He is now a PE teacher in Wishaw.

Games:	48
Goals:	5
Born:	Falkirk

WILSON WOOD
1963–67

A talented left-half who was never a first-team regular but had considerable ability, Wood suffered from being a contemporary of Jim Baxter, and many friends of Rangers felt that he should have been encouraged positively and groomed to be Baxter's successor in season 1965–66, when he managed only eleven games. He was one of the few players to have played in all three Scottish derby games, in Glasgow, Edinburgh and Dundee. He went to Dundee United with Davie Wilson in August 1967, in exchange for Orjan Persson. Wood has developed his own physiotherapy practice in Whitburn.

Games:	47
Goals:	4
Born:	Whitburn

JORN SORENSEN
1965–66

A Danish player from Morton, Jorn arrived at Ibrox in August 1965 in exchange for winger Craig Watson and a fee of around £12,000. He was a talented midfield player of high class, in the manner of Ian McMillan. He was approaching the veteran stage when signed by Rangers and the pace of the modern game was probably a problem for him, although his skills and European experience might have been better used helping young wingers like Willie Johnston. At the end of his one season, he went back to Denmark.

Games:	16
Goals:	3
Honours:	31 Denmark caps (none with Rangers)
Born:	Nibe, Denmark, 17 October 1936

WILLIE MATHIESON
1964–75

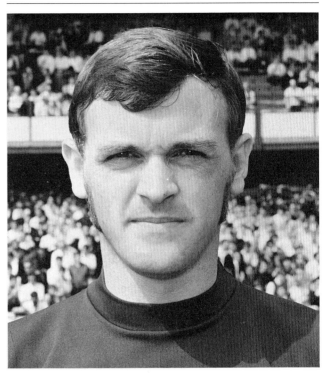

Dubbed Willie 'Wan Fit' (one foot) by Rangers fans, Mathieson, a left-back, was certainly partial to the use of his left foot and was much maligned for it. Since Mathieson had an eleven-year stay at the club, this criticism was evidently over-dramatic and less than fair. Willie, from St Andrews United, was a perfectly good attacking full-back, and comparing him with predecessors like Eric Caldow and John Little was unacceptable. 'Jardine and Mathieson' was a successful and established full-back partnership for a goodly spell. Willie was in the European Cup Winners' Cup team of 1972 and played for the Scottish League, and successive Rangers managers Symon, Waddell, White and Wallace all thought him good enough to play in what were good Rangers teams during his time at Ibrox. He finished his playing days with Raith Rovers.

Games:	274
Goals:	3
European Cup Winners' Cup:	1971–72
Scottish Cup:	1972–73
Born:	St Andrews, 20 January 1943

KAI JOHANSEN
1965–70

A Danish international full-back of outstanding talent, Kai Johansen was signed from Morton on 24 June 1965 for £20,000. This was at a time when Hal Stewart, the Morton impresario, was importing Scandinavian players galore. A right-back who could also play comfortably on the left, Kai took a little time to adjust to life at Ibrox, to some extent because of the restrictions Scot Symon sought to inflict on his play. Symon did not believe that defenders, and certainly not full-backs, should cross the halfway line. Johansen was a modern, attacking full-back, highly regarded throughout Europe with his crouching style, attacking the ball and coming forward at speed. He entered Rangers folklore in the Rangers–Celtic Scottish Cup Final of 1966. The first match was drawn 0–0 and Johansen had a hard time against John Hughes, the big Celtic outside-left. In the replay, by contrast, he had Hughes 'in his pocket' and ennobled himself by scoring the only goal, a cracking low drive from 25 yards after seventy minutes' play.

Johansen was a prodigious talker – couldn't be stopped. He ran a pub in Glasgow, retired in 1970, then had a pub on Spain's Costa del Sol. Back in Denmark he became a.player's agent, and he operated for a spell in South Africa.

Games:	238
Goals:	9
Scottish Cup:	1965–66
Honours	20 Denmark caps (none with Rangers)
Born:	Odense, Denmark, 23 February 1940

WILLIE JOHNSTON
1964–73, 1980–82

One of the most controversial footballers of modern times, Willie Johnston was an outside-left of blistering pace, dazzling dribbling skills and the highest international qualities, but he may be better remembered for an appalling disciplinary record and for being banned from the international game following a drugs test at the World Championship in Argentina in 1978. Johnston was ordered off at least twenty times in his career.

From the junior Lochore Welfare in Fife, 'Bud' Johnston signed for Rangers in 1964. He made his debut, aged seventeen, in a League match at home to St Johnstone on 29 August that year, and two months later played in the final, one of the more memorable Rangers–Celtic matches which Rangers won 2–1. So hugely skilled was Johnston that he progressed from Scottish youth international to full international status in six months, and was first capped at eighteen in a World Cup qualifying match. He played well, but it was not the happiest of starts. Poland at Hampden scored two goals in the last five minutes to win 2–1. But Johnston was a regular international player from then on.

He played at inside-left early in his career, making a devastating wing partnership with Davie Wilson, whose maturity and experience brought the young man along nicely. Johnston was an entertainer. His speed, strength and commanding skills with the ball gave him a rapport with the fans. He could be argumentative, and was, clearly too often with referees. He was something of an expert at football quizzes, which he would organise on the team bus, and over the facts he would tussle with anyone. But Rangers tired of his lack of on-field discipline. His last suspension, a nine-week sentence following an ordering-off offence against Partick Thistle on 9 September 1972, led to his transfer to West Bromwich Albion for £135,000 on 1 December that year. Just six months earlier he had been a European Cup Winners' Cup medal winner, scoring two of Rangers' three goals in the final against Moscow Dynamo in Barcelona. Indeed, Johnston goals had been instrumental in taking Rangers to that final; his four goals included vital away scores at Rennes and Turin.

'Bud' and Colin Stein seemed to be the prima donnas of the Ibrox dressing room. Perhaps the new regime of Jock Wallace after 1972 was too harsh for them (Stein was sold to Coventry City on 5 October 1972 for £90,000 and the former Ayr United winger Quinton Young). A Wallace remark when Johnston and Stein had gone was telling – he said, 'We have sold two stars and found a team.'

Johnston played well at West Bromwich and was brought into the squad of Scotland players for the World Championship finals in Argentina. Following the match against Peru (lost 3–1) he was routinely tested and found to have taken a banned substance. He was withdrawn from the tournament, sent home and banned from playing for Scotland ever again. The Scottish Football Association declared that it had been plain stupidity on Johnston's part. All the Scotland players had been asked, both collectively and individually, "Have you taken any substance AT ALL, since you came here?" In every case, they said, the answer was no. Needless to say, Johnston had another version, published in a later book, in which he claimed that the Scotland team doctor Fitzsimmons had cleared the pills beforehand! He also claimed that the substance in question, 'Reactivan", was freely available to the public in the UK and had been taken by many members of the squad. Wherever the truth lay, Johnston's international career was over.

He went to Vancouver Whitecaps in March, 1979, played with Birmingham City on loan, came back to Rangers for manager John Greig in August 1980, and played with some distinction during two more years with the club. His first match was on August 16, at home to Partick Thistle. A month later, in a League Cup match against Aberdeen at Ibrox, Willie Johnston was – ordered off! He played finally with Hearts and Falkirk, retiring only in his 39th year, in 1985.

Games:	393
Goals:	126
Scottish Cup:	1965–66
League Cup:	1964–65, 70–71
European Cup Winners' Cup:	1971–72
Honours:	22 Scotland caps (9 with Rangers)
Born:	Glasgow, 19 December 1946

THEROLF BECK
1964–65

Therolf Beck from Iceland, known affectionately as 'Totty' Beck, which was as close as Glasgow cared to come to pronouncing his Christian name, was signed from St Mirren on 11 November 1964 for £20,000, perhaps because he had lately played very well against Rangers. Such performances often impressed them. But Totty, an inside-left, was not a success. There was a suspicion that the Rangers ambiance and the city lights were too much for him, and he went back to Iceland.

Games:	14
Goals	2
Born:	Reykjavik, Iceland

DENIS SETTERINGTON
1965–70

A fringe player of the late sixties, Denis was an inside-forward or midfield player who looked as though he might become very good, but who was hindered by injuries. He moved to Falkirk for £10,000.

Games:	14
Goals:	5
Born:	Edinburgh

BILLY PAUL
1966–67

An outside-right with limited opportunities, he played only part of one game.

Games:	1
Goals:	0
Born:	Glasgow

BOBBY WATSON
1964–70

Bobby Watson came out of Airdrie Schools football and as a right-half or inside-right was technically very sound, hard-working, whole-hearted and an effective tackler in midfield. He arrived in the post-Baxter and McMillan days, and found John Greig taking the right-half position, under Davie White's management. He played inside-right with distinction in the Scottish Cup Final matches against Celtic in 1966. Watson was badly injured in a bad tackle from Lothar Emmerich, the West German international, after forty minutes' play against Borussia in Dortmund in a European Cup Winners' Cup match of season 1966–67.

He moved to Motherwell in 1970 with Brian Herron in exchange for goalkeeper Peter McCloy, became captain there and probably had his best seasons at Fir Park. He later became manager of Motherwell, and also of Airdrie. Always very articulate, Bobby Watson was a lay preacher, was successful in the steel business, and in the late eighties was on the board of Partick Thistle as part of a group seeking to revive the club.

Games:	82
Goals:	7
Scottish Cup:	1965–66
Born:	Airdrie, May 1946

COLIN JACKSON
1963–82

Colin Macdonald Jackson was a centre-half who gave Rangers twenty seasons of sterling service. He was tall and slender, of no great physique, yet he was an excellent stopper and a perceptive penalty-area player who could deny strikers space to move and manoeuvre. He was marvellously dependable, particularly in the air. He was also very patient, spending much time in reserve to Ronnie McKinnon and even Derek Johnstone. The greatest disappointment of his career must have been failing a fitness test on the eve of the European final of 1972 at Barcelona. He had played a significant role in getting Rangers to that final. Perhaps one of the highlights of his career was in the dying moments of the 1978–79 League Cup Final against Aberdeen – he headed the winning goal from a corner kick in the ninetieth minute!

Rangers had signed him from Sunnybank Athletic in Aberdeen, from under the noses of the Pittodrie scouting staff. Colin was born in London. He, Richard Gough and John Little are the only Rangers players born outside the country and capped for Scotland.

Games:	506
Goals:	40
League Championship:	1974–75, 75–76, 77–78
Scottish Cup:	1975–76, 77–78, 78–79
League Cup:	1970–71, 75–76, 77–78, 78–79, 81–82
Honours:	8 Scotland caps
Born:	London, 8 October 1946

DAVE SMITH
1966–74

A superb, cultured left-half, Dave was already an international player when Rangers signed him from Aberdeen on 12 August 1966 for £50,000. He was an elegant player, a beautiful stylist whose cool positional sense and anticipation, as well as his precise passing of the ball, made him one of the outstanding players in the Scottish game of his time. He could also play very effectively as a sweeper, which he did in Rangers' victory over Moscow Dynamo in the European Cup Winners' Cup Final in 1972, when he won his only medal during his time at Ibrox. He succeeded Jim Baxter, but never quite had the acclaim he should have had. He certainly should have played more often for Scotland. He was a brother of Doug Smith, long-time (1958–76) centre-half of Dundee United and now a director of that club. Dave Smith moved to Arbroath on 4 November 1974 for £12,000, becoming player–coach. He was later player–manager of Berwick Rangers and Peterhead, and played in Los Angeles for the Aztecs and in South Africa.

Games:	300
Goals:	13
European Cup Winners' Cup:	1971–72
Honours:	2 Scotland caps
	(1 with Rangers)
Born:	Aberdeen, 14 November
	1943

ALEC SMITH
1966–69

Alec Smith, no relation to Dave, was signed just three days before he was, from Dunfermline Athletic for £55,000. A droll tale hangs on this transfer. It seems that the Dunfermline chairman asked his manager, Willie Cunningham, how much they might get for Smith. 'Lucky to get £25,000' was the reply. However, Cunningham gave Scot Symon a big speech about what a good player Smith was, how many clubs were chasing him, and so on. Symon said he'd make a formal offer in writing. A few days later, Cunningham had a letter and an offer – of £55,000. Almost like the blind auction in Scottish property buying.

Smith was a good player, very able in the air, intelligent, strong, a right-half or inside-forward whose forte was strength on the ball and in breaking forward, but his major drawback was a lack of pace. He moved on to Aberdeen in June 1969. One of the mysteries of this mysterious game came in the dying moments of the 1966–67 League Cup Final against Celtic when the experienced Smith, only a few yards from goal with Celtic goalkeeper Ronnie Simpson beaten and the goal unguarded, unaccountably stumbled and Billy McNeill was able to make a clearance.
Celtic won 1–0.

Games:	68
Goals:	26
Born:	St Andrews
Dunfermline Scottish Cup:	1960–61

BILLY SEMPLE
1967–72

A dark, strongly built lad, Billy was an outside-left who was in and out of the team when wingers like Wilson, Johnston and Persson were on the books. He was a lively extrovert on the team bus, doing impressions of Billy Connolly, Chick Murray and others. He was given a free transfer in May 1972.

Games:	9
Goals:	2
Born:	Bellshill, 2 November 1946

SANDY JARDINE
1965–82

William Pullar Jardine, nicknamed 'Sandy' because of the colour of his hair, was one of the finest Rangers players in the entire post-war era. He was a cultured, elegant footballer, cool, strong, very fast, scrupulously fair. Originally a wing-half, he played there, at midfield, as a sweeper and full-back, and even as centre-forward for a spell under Davie White's management. He was developed by Willie Waddell as a full-back and could play comfortably on either side. Sandy came to Rangers from Edinburgh minor football – he lived quite near the Hearts ground – and he made his debut at eighteen in the week after the 'Berwick Disaster' of January 1967. That was against Hearts, of all people, at Ibrox. Rangers won 5–1.

In his international debut, against Portugal at Hampden in 1971, he marked Eusebio out of the game, and after the European final in Nuremberg in l967 he was much praised by his opposite number, Franz Beckenbauer. He was in the Rangers team which eventually did win the European Cup Winners' Cup, in Barcelona in 1972. At his best, Jardine was certainly a world-class player. He and Danny McGrain of Celtic formed a first-class partnership for Scotland as the full-back pairing on nineteen occasions. He played in the World Cup Finals in Germany in 1974 and Argentina in 1978, and captained Rangers for a spell. He was one of the few players to be twice voted the sports writers' Player of the Year.

Sandy was released by John Greig after the Scottish Cup Final of 1982, at the age of thirty-three, and he joined Hearts where he had a marvellous Indian summer to his career, bringing his lifetime appearance total in all matches to more than a thousand. As sweeper, he was a mainstay of the 1985–86 team which came so close to doing a Scottish 'double' but finished second in both League and Scottish Cup. He became assistant manager to Alex Macdonald, then joint manager before leaving Hearts in 1988.

Games:	671
Goals:	76
League Championship:	1974–75, 75–76, 77–78
Scottish Cup:	1972–73, 75–76, 77–78, 78–79, 80–81
League Cup:	1970–71, 75–76, 77–78, 78–79, 81–82
European Cup Winners' Cup:	1971–72
Honours:	38 Scotland caps
Born:	Edinburgh, 31 December1948

ERIC SORENSEN
1967–70

The 'Man in Black' was bought from Morton on 26 July 1967 for £25,000. This was Eric Sorensen, Danish international goalkeeper brought over by Hal Stewart, the Morton boss and impresario who was conducting at the time a policy of importing leading Scandinavian players. For publicity reasons, Stewart kept Sorensen's identity unknown until he made his debut, but compounded the mystery by calling him simply the 'Man in Black', from the all-black strip which he wore. There was nothing extraordinary in the uniform – all continental goalkeepers wore black in the days before their present multi-coloured strips became fashionable.

Sorensen turned out to be a spectacular, top-class goalkeeper who played a full season in the first team. He made his debut on 12 August in a League Cup tie against Aberdeen at Pittodrie (1–1), and played his last match, also against Aberdeen, at Ibrox on 27 April 1968 (Aberdeen won 3–2 with a goal in the very last minute). It was Rangers' only League defeat; they amassed their highest points total since Scottish League reconstruction twelve years earlier, yet they still lost the Championship to Celtic by two points!

Perhaps a combination of ill-luck, misfortune or whatever meant that the blond, blue-eyed Sorensen never quite became the darling of the Ibrox fans. He remained at the club for two more years without ever playing another first-team match, then left on the same day, 28 April 1970, as his rival Norrie Martin, with whom he had contested the position. He went back to Morton, where he recovered his poise and played successfully for a few more seasons. He later took a pub in Greenock, and, a keen student of the game, became a goalkeeping coach working with, among others, Alan Rough.

Games:	48
Shutouts:	16
Honours:	15 Denmark caps (none with Rangers)
Born:	Odense, Denmark, 22 January 1940

ORJAN PERSSON
1967–70

More mature Rangers fans will relish the memory of one particular Persson goal, the one that produced the first defeat of Celtic's post-Lisbon team. At Ibrox in September 1967, before a crowd of 90,000 (!), Persson, two minutes into the second half, set off on a mazy run of thirty yards or so, taking him past player after player in the Celtic defence. Then, from a near-impossible angle, he sliced his left-foot shot past Ronnie Simpson. Persson was something of a specialist in making the ball move through the air, swerving, curling and slicing it, particularly dangerously from free kicks, even corner kicks.

He was a Swedish international signed from Dundee United in exchange for Davie Wilson and Wilson Wood, a hugely talented if inconsistent player who could score, it seemed, from any angle, any position. Another of his goals was a scissors kick from twenty-five yards which gave Rangers a 1–1 draw with Hearts in a Scottish Cup tie. Orjan played for Sweden in the World Championship finals of 1970 in Mexico, while still a Rangers player. Later that year he went to Orgryte in Sweden for a small fee.

Games:	112
Goals:	31
Honours:	48 Sweden caps (6 with Rangers)
Born:	Sweden, 27 August 1942

ANDY PENMAN
1967–73

When Andy Penman arrived at Ibrox in April 1967 from Dundee, in exchange for George McLean and £30,000, Rangers had acquired a mature international player who could boast of an extraordinary career. Penman had been something of a boy prodigy. From Dunfermline Schools he had gone to Everton, making his debut there in a Lancashire Senior Cup match against Liverpool at the age of fifteen. Back in Dundee, he made his debut for them when not quite sixteen and still an amateur. He was capped for Scotland at schoolboy, youth, amateur (probably the youngest-ever amateur player for Scotland), Under-23 and senior levels. He won a League Championship with Dundee in 1961–62, and played in a Scottish Cup Final (in 1964, against Rangers) before coming to Ibrox where, surprisingly, and like Orjan Persson, he won nothing at all.

Andy Penman was a midfield player of class and startling vision, a fine passer of the ball who could clip balls precisely through, round and over defences to give his forwards clear, untrammelled runs at goal. In the Scottish Cup Final of 1971 against Celtic, he carved openings time and again only for Willie Johnston and Colin Stein to spurn them. Fitness and health were problems for Andy – he was prone to put on weight, and he was a diabetic. He used dead-ball situations to telling effect, and in a better Rangers team (Rangers in his time, the late sixties, were always chasing and struggling against Celtic) he could have been one of the historically memorable Rangers players. In 1973 he moved to Arbroath, in 1976 to Inverness Caley, and in 1979 he retired.

Games:	150
Goals:	49
Honours:	3 Scotland caps (2 with Rangers)
Born:	Rosyth, 20 February 1943
Dundee League Championship:	1961–62

ALEX FERGUSON
1967–69

One of the most consistently controversial figures in football over the past twenty-five years, Alex Ferguson is the local boy who made more than good. Brought up in Govan, the Rangers heartland, he was 'Rangers-daft' in boyhood. At Queen's Park in the late fifties, he played for Scotland Youth as a rip-roaring centre-forward. In 1960 he joined St Johnstone, and in 1964 he was bought by Dunfermline, a transfer justified by his tally of sixty-six goals in eighty-eight League games in a team that missed winning the Championship of 1964–65 by a single point. He was signed by Rangers for £65,000 in July 1967.

In his first season at Ibrox, Alex was leading scorer with nineteen goals from twenty-nine League matches. Ferguson was lean and hard, a hustling, bustling, elbows-out striker, uncompromising and rumbustious. Defenders became nervous when Alex was about, and he and Colin Stein formed a powerful attacking force for Rangers. He left the club following a row with Davie White, the manager, over the 1969 Scottish Cup Final. That was the match in which Billy McNeill, the Celtic centre-half, unmarked, headed in a Bobby Lennox corner kick after just two minutes' play. Celtic went on to overwhelm Rangers 4–0. White insisted that Ferguson should have been marking McNeill. He moved to Falkirk in November 1969 for £20,000, and was in their promotion team the following season. At Falkirk he played beside Andy Roxburgh – both men were to become Scotland team managers. After four years with Falkirk and one with Ayr United, Alex was forced to retire because of injuries.

He then learned the management game with East Stirlingshire, and in taking St Mirren into the Premier Division before going on to Aberdeen with the avowed ambition of 'smashing' the Old Firm hegemony. He did it by going on the attack in the citadels of Ibrox and Parkhead. The result was vigorous matches and for Aberdeen three Championship, four Scottish Cup and one League Cup victories and one European title in Ferguson's time at the club – an exceptional achievement. In 1983 he turned down an invitation to manage Rangers when John Greig left, and he became Scotland team manager on a temporary basis for the World Championships final competition in Mexico following the death of Jock Stein. He was appointed manager of Manchester United in November 1986.

Games:	67
Goals:	35
Born:	Glasgow

COLIN STEIN
1968–73, 1975–77

Colin was signed from Hibernian in October 1968 for £100,000, the first six-figure transfer between Scottish clubs. A product of Linlithgow Schools football, he was almost an 'old-fashioned' centre-forward, strong, bustling, with rather a short fuse; his temperament saw him sent off several times in his career. His impact on the club was immediate. He scored a hat-trick in his opening games, at Arbroath and at home to Hibernian, and that meant instant popularity with the Ibrox crowd. He scored four goals in a World Cup qualifying match against Cyprus in May 1969. He was not the cleverest player in football but, blond and busy, Colin would simply hammer the most meagre of chances at goal, from any range. He scored in Rangers' European Cup Winners' Cup success in Barcelona in 1972.

In October of that year he was transferred to Coventry City for £90,000 plus Quinton Young, former Ayr United winger, and after some initial success there he came back to Rangers in February 1975 when it appeared that Coventry could no longer maintain the transfer instalments. His 'second coming' was restricted by the presence of the two Dereks, Johnstone and Parlane, but he did score a critical goal, his first since returning to the club, at Easter Road. It was an equaliser that gave Rangers a draw and their first Championship win in eleven years. On loan to Kilmarnock in season 1977–78, Colin Stein was given a free transfer at the end of that season.

Games:	206
Goals:	97
League Cup:	1970–71, 75–76
European Cup Winners' Cup:	1971–72
Honours:	21 Scotland caps (17 with Rangers)
Born:	Philipstoun, West Lothian, 10 May 1947

ALEX MacDONALD
1968–81

One of Rangers' most valuable signings, Alex Macdonald's long career at Ibrox began with his transfer from St Johnstone, for £50,000, on 19 November 1968. Alex took a little time to settle at Ibrox and was not immediately accepted by the fans. But playing as a left-side midfield player, or inside-forward, he became the powerhouse of a Rangers team that was immensely successful through the seventies. Fiery, red-haired, small, combative, a ball-winner and a great competitor, Alex eventually became overwhelmingly popular with the fans, who dubbed him 'Doddie'. He was adept at stealing into the blind side of opposing defences and snatching important goals, never more so than the solitary winning goal he headed against Celtic in the 1975–76 League Cup Final. Alex was in Rangers' winning team in the European Cup Winners' Cup Final of 1972. He moved to Hearts in August 1980, became player–manager in 1981, then took over as manager where his ability and energy brought him the award of Manager of the Year in 1986.

Games:	500
Goals:	92
League Championship:	1974–75, 75–76, 77–78
Scottish Cup:	1972–73, 75–76, 77–78, 78–79
League Cup:	1970–71, 75–76, 77–78, 78–79
European Cup Winners' Cup:	1971–72
Honours:	1 Scotland cap
Born:	Glasgow, 17 March 1948

GERRY NEEF
1967–73

The German goalkeeper, possibly the only German who ever played for Rangers, had had trials with Aberdeen before coming to Ibrox in the spring of 1968. Gerhard's first match was at home to Morton on 19 April 1969 (3–0) and he kept his place for most of season 1969–70 until the coming of Peter McCloy from Motherwell in March 1970. He was on the bench as a substitute in Barcelona in 1972 for Rangers' successful European Cup Winners' Cup Final against Moscow Dynamo.

He took a good deal of ribbing in the Ibrox dressing room because of his nationality, but he gave as good as he got, and was a popular lad. At 5'10" and of slender build, he was never very big for a goalkeeper, but he had exceptional agility.

Games: 48
Shutouts: 17
Born: Hausham, West Germany, 30 December 1946

ALFIE CONN
1968–74

Alfred James Conn was the son of a famous father, Alfie Conn, the international inside-right of the famous Conn–Bauld–Wardhaugh attacking trio in an excellent Hearts team of the forties and early fifties. Thus the young man reached senior level from a family background and environment which left him steeped in the game, and he was bursting with natural talent and confidence. Almost inevitably, he was an international player at schoolboy, youth, Under-23 and senior levels. Alfie was a right-side player with, like his father, a tremendous shot in his right foot. He played his first match for the club in Dundalk in November 1968, in what was then the 'Fairs Cities Cup'. Affected by injuries intermittently throughout his career, he was in Rangers' European Cup Winners' Cup team, a winning team, in Barcelona 1972. One of his more memorable goals was Rangers' second in their 3–2 Scottish Cup win in 1973, when his run on goal exposed the lack of pace of Billy McNeill, the Celtic centre-half.

Conn moved to Tottenham Hotspur in July 1974 for £140,000 and was capped while at White Hart Lane. Alfie committed the ultimate sin in March 1977 by signing for Celtic in a £65,000 transfer and to this day has never been forgiven by Rangers supporters. In 1977 he made history by appearing in a winning Celtic team in a Scottish Cup Final against Rangers. Thus he had played for both Old Firm clubs against the other in winning Scottish Cup Final sides. He was with Pittsburgh in 1979, Hearts in 80–81, then with Blackpool and Motherwell.

Games:	146
Goals:	39
Scottish Cup:	1972–73
League Cup:	1970–71
European Cup Winners' Cup:	1971–72
Honours:	2 Scotland caps (none with Rangers)
Born:	Kirkcaldy, 5 April 1952
Celtic	
Scottish Cup:	1976–77

BRIAN HERON
1969–70

Outside-left was Brian's original position, but he was converted to left-back during Davie White's last season at Ibrox, for his only lengthy spell in the team. Brian went to Motherwell with Bobby Watson in exchange for Peter McCloy.

Games:	9
Goals:	0
Born:	Glasgow

BILLY McPHEE
1968–70

Inside-forward, fringe player who never found a regular place.

Games:	3
Goals:	0
Born:	Methil

WILLIE WHITE
1969–70

Another young full-back of great but unfulfilled promise. His one game was against Airdrie in 1970, at right-back partnering Davie Provan to a 1–1 draw.

Games: 1
Goals: 0
Born: Irvine

KENNY WATSON (1)
1969–71

A powerful left-side player who had played for Scotland Youth before joining Rangers, Kenny had a fierce shot and showed much early promise. A weight problem was one of the factors that prevented his obvious promise from maturing.

Games: 4
Goals: 0
Born: Edinburgh

IAIN MacDONALD
1969–73

An outside-left in the mould of Willie Johnston and Willie Henderson, Iain showed great talent as a youngster, breaking into the team under Willie Waddell in 1969–70. A cartilage operation in March 1970 ended that season for him, and after a spell with Dundee United injuries forced him to give up the game.

Games: 14
Goals: 2
Born: Edinburgh, 26 August 1952

PETER McCLOY
1970–86

At 6' 4" beyond much doubt the tallest goalkeeper in British football in his time, Peter McCloy was dubbed the 'Girvan Lighthouse' after his coastal birthplace in Ayrshire. The son of a St Mirren goalkeeper, he began his senior career with Motherwell in 1964. In exchange for Bobby Watson and Brian Heron, he moved to Rangers in the spring of 1970, towards the end of what had been a rather barren season for the Ibrox club. Indeed in McCloy's first match, Rangers were beaten 2–1 at Dunfermline. But for the next four seasons, he made the position his own. He was capped by Scotland and won his share of honours with the club, notably a place in the European Cup Winners' Cup Final of 1972, when Rangers beat Moscow Dynamo in Barcelona. He played a record number of games for a Rangers goalkeeper, 644 in all, thus passing the mark of 545 which the famous Jerry Dawson had set between 1929 and 1945.

In international terms, Peter was contemporary with Alistair Hunter of Kilmarnock and Celtic, David Harvey of Leeds United, Bobby Clark of Aberdeen and later, Alan Rough of Partick Thistle – formidable opposition. And when Stewart Kennedy joined Rangers in 1973, he and McCloy fought over the position for some four years. McCloy was the better survivor and was mainly in possession from 1978 to 1981. Then Jim Stewart, yet another international player, arrived in March of 1981 and McCloy had a battle on his hands yet again. Yet again he prevailed, at least until the coming of Graeme Souness and Chris Woods in 1986. Then Peter became a coach at Ibrox and subsequently became a freelance coach, working with Hearts and other clubs.

His height, of course, was a prodigious advantage with high crosses and lobs, although he would sometimes slap at balls rather than punch or catch. His huge downfield clearances became an attacking gambit for Rangers, in particular when Derek Johnstone, a target for the kicks, was playing in attack. It has often been claimed that Peter was capped for Scotland at golf. Not so – another myth has to be exploded, even if Peter was a first-class player. The Scottish Golf Union has no record of a Peter McCloy having played, at boy, youth or senior level.

Games:	533
Shutouts:	214
League Championship:	1975–76
Scottish Cup:	1972–73, 75–76, 77–78, 78–79
League Cup:	1970–71, 78–79, 83–84, 84–85
European Cup Winners' Cup:	1971–72
Honours:	4 Scotland caps
Born:	Girvan, 16 November 1946

GRAHAM FYFE
1969–76

Graham played in almost all the forward positions for Rangers, and was a very skilful, very talented player even if he held a place in the team only intermittently. He was a very clever ball-player and an old-fashioned dribbler of the ball, and fitfully would play quite spectacular games, scoring spectacular goals. One of these games, including a cracking goal, came in a 'Juan Gamper' tournament in Barcelona which had the local press comparing him to his opposite number in the Barcelona team, one Johan Cruyff.

For long spells in the Jock Wallace reign he was the regular substitute, rather like David Fairclough at Liverpool, a role he performed successfully, often coming on to score decisive goals. Unpredictable and inconsistent, Graham went to Hibs in 1976 with Alistair Scott in exchange for Iain Munro. His career there was no different.

However, in later years he created great controversy with his statements on why he had left Ibrox. On the age-old topic of Rangers' policy with regard to employing Roman Catholic players, the media in the mid eighties highlighted cases where Rangers players had married Catholic girls, and tried to persuade them to admit that this had affected their careers. They approached three players in particular. Robert Russell told them point-blank that it had not affected his career (he went on to play several more seasons at the club). Derek Johnstone quite simply refused to discuss it, declining to be interviewed or quoted, but within three months of having married he had been made club captain. Graham Fyfe, on the other hand, said that he was absolutely certain that the real reason he could not get a regular place at Ibrox was because he had married a Catholic girl. Despite the furore it caused at the time, and regular rumblings since then, Rangers' signing of Maurice Johnstone in 1989 has surely put an end to such nonsense.

Games: 87
Goals: 31
Born: Motherwell, 18 August 1951

ANGUS McCALLUM
1970–71

A Scottish Youth centre-half known as 'Gus', who did not develop to Rangers' requirements.

Games:	1
Goals:	0
Born:	Glasgow, 19 March 1953

TOM ALEXANDER
1970–73

Tall, slim, another promising young full-back earning only minimal exposure.

Games:	2
Goals:	0
Born:	Ayr, 20 October 1951

R.M. WATSON
1970–73

Goalkeeper Bobby Watson had a meteoric start to his Ibrox career. Signed from Ardrossan Winton Rovers in July 1970, having had an outstanding career in junior football, he made his first-team debut that same month, coming on as a substitute for Gerry Neef in a pre-season friendly in Hamburg. He retained his place in further matches against Kaiserslautern and Tottenham Hotspur and played in the opening League Cup match, against Dunfermline Athletic at Ibrox on August 8, 1970. After a 1-3 Glasgow Cup Final defeat at the hands of Celtic two days later, Watson was dropped and never again played in the first team. He was released at the end of season 1972–73.

Games:	1
Shutouts:	0
Born:	Glasgow, 22 March 1950

JIM DENNY
1970–79

Membership of a unique club came to Jim Denny with his very first game for Rangers. It was the Scottish Cup Final of 1971, and Jim thus emulated a predecessor, Willie Reid, who had done exactly the same more than sixty years earlier. (This was perhaps the only similiarity in their careers.) Denny played right-back in the replay, which Celtic won 2–1, and although a novice aged twenty-one, played perfectly well and was not responsible for the defeat. He was in the team because Rangers had something of an injury crisis.

Jim was versatile. He played in every position for Rangers, including goalkeeper, mainly in the reserves. He was of medium height, medium build, medium ability. His club-mates cynically called him 'Pelé' because of his lack of ball control, and he was something of a utility, or even fringe, player. But he did play in Europe more than once, for example in Cologne in 1979, listed as outside-left. He moved to Hearts on a £30,000 transfer on 4 September 1979.

Games:	66
Goals:	0
Born:	Paisley, 13 March 1950

DEREK PARLANE
1970–80

Son of the former Rangers inside-forward Jimmy Parlane, Derek James Parlane was a midfield player converted into a centre-forward by Jock Wallace. Tall, strong and energetic, Derek made a success of the move. In four seasons out of five he was leading goal-scorer, despite being a contemporary of Derek Johnstone for much of the time. He was particularly strong in the air, and an invaluable attacking force for both Rangers and Scotland. Willie Waddell and Willie Thornton together had gone down to the village of Rhu on the Clyde estuary to sign him as a teenager, against very strong competition from many clubs, when he was a Queen's Park player.

He impressed himself on a wider audience in the European Cup Winners' Cup semi-final of 1972, against Bayern Munich, when he replaced the injured John Greig at right-half. Parlane played 'the game of his life', volleying home a Willie Johnston corner kick for Rangers' second goal. Derek scored Rangers' 6000th League goal against Hearts at Tynecastle on 19 January 1974, scoring all four goals in a 4–2 victory. He was transferred to Leeds United in March 1980 for £160,000 and after playing successfully there, he moved on to Manchester City in July 1983. He later played for Swansea Town, and after retiring in 1985 he became a director of non-league club Macclesfield Town, while in business in Cheshire.

Games:	296
Goals:	111
League Championship:	1974–75, 75–76, 77–78
Scottish Cup:	1972–73, 78–79
League Cup:	1975–76, 77–78, 78–79
Honours:	12 Scotland caps
Born:	Helensburgh, 5 May 1953

ALEX MILLER
1967–83

Alex came from Clydebank Juniors in 1967. A centre-forward, he scored goals galore in the reserve team, but developed as a full-back and indeed played many positions in a long career with the club. He may very well have suffered from this versatility. When the present principles of substitution were established, Alex became the ideal 'sub'. Tall and slim, Miller was not over-skilled but he was sure and steadfast and always produced a thoroughly reliable game. He was an expert penalty-scorer, the best Rangers had had since Johnny Hubbard. Alex was popular, rather quiet, an altogether nice man and dedicated to the cause. He played the entire Scottish Cup Final of 1971 despite having suffered a broken jaw in the first half. In the middle seventies he played well enough to keep Sandy Jardine out of the team for a spell. He was released by John Greig, and quickly built a successful management career in turn with Morton, St Mirren and finally Hibernian.

Games:	305
Goals:	30
League Championship:	1974–75, 75–76, 77–78
Scottish Cup:	1975–76, 78–79
League Cup:	1970–71, 77–78, 78–79, 81–82
Born:	Glasgow, 7 April 1949

DEREK JOHNSTONE
1970–83, 1985–86

Derek Johnstone has been arguably the most versatile player the club has ever had in the post-war era. In an outstanding career he played at centre-half, in midfield and at centre-forward for the club. He also played for Scotland in all three sections of the team and believes he is the only man to have done that. He scored the only goal, the winning goal in the 1970–71 League Cup Final in his first Old Firm match. He was 16 years and 355 days old, the youngest footballer surely ever to have scored the winning goal in a national cup final. Jock Wallace, then the coach at Ibrox, can take some of the credit: he insisted that the young Johnstone be selected. It was Rangers' first trophy in five years. Johnstone went on to score 131 League goals, a post-war Rangers record in the days before Alistair McCoist, and for these facts alone his place in the lore of the club is secure.

He was something of a boy wonder. A product of Dundee Schools football, he played for Scotland at schoolboy, youth, amateur, Under-23 and senior international level. His first love was Dundee United, and he trained with them for a spell but found their methods monotonous. He signed schoolboy forms for Rangers in December 1968 and a full professional contract in July 1970. Derek was a big lad, six feet tall and powerfully built even then. He played his first match on 19 September 1970 against Cowdenbeath at Ibrox. Rangers won 5–0 and young Johnstone had two of the goals. The 'immortal' goal, in the League Cup Final, came only one month later. From then on Derek was seldom out of the team.

His club record was outstanding. He won Scottish Cup medals in three different positions; he scored goals in Scottish Cup Finals from both centre-half and centre-forward positions. Centre-half was his favoured position. He was and certainly deserved to be compared to the fabled John Charles of Wales in his physical power, his exceptional heading abilities, his nimbleness and quickness over the ground for such a big man, and as a goal-scorer. Johnstone by any standard was an exceptional player. As a centre-forward he scored dozens of goals with his head, mainly from the precise crosses of Tommy McLean on the right wing, and since he did little roaming to the wings, he forced many goals at close range in the goal area.

He was a member of the Scotland international squad for the World Championships of 1978 in Argentina but was not selected to play in any of the matches, an omission that was condemned by the Rangers faithful, and others, as a fatal error of judgement and a tactical disaster on the part of the team manager, Alistair McLeod. Certainly Johnstone had scored in two of the three preceding international matches.

Derek's later years at Ibrox seemed dogged with problems. John Greig, on becoming manager, made him club captain, but Johnstone for some reason was not completely happy and three years later asked to be relieved of it. Many Rangers fans felt that Johnstone's considerable abilities had not been used to the full. The signing by Greig of Colin MacAdam from Partick Thistle in 1980, who was preferred to Johnstone as a centre-forward although he had much less talent, was a straw in the wind of change. The manager's decision to leave out 'D.J.', David Cooper and John Macdonald was seen as a serious tactical error when the 1981 Scottish Cup Final with Dundee United proved a dull goalless draw. These three players transformed the replay; Rangers played their finest football in years and won 4–1 with Johnstone outstanding at centre-forward.

He eventually left in 1983, transferring to Chelsea for £30,000. He played on loan for Dundee United for one month in October 1983 before Jock Wallace, now Rangers' manager, re-signed him in January 1985 for £25,000. His second stint at Ibrox was not a success; he had increasing weight problems, and he was freed by Graeme Souness in 1986. After a brief spell as manager of Partick Thistle, he joined Radio Clyde. An extrovert with a sharp sense of humour and fun, broadcasting may well be an ideal second career for 'D.J.'.

Games:	547
Goals:	209
League Championship:	74–75, 75–76, 77–78
Scottish Cup:	1972–73, 75–76, 77–78, 78–79, 80–81
League Cup:	1970–71, 75–76, 77–78, 78–79, 81–82
European Cup Winners' Cup:	1972
Honours:	14 Scotland caps
Born:	Dundee, 4 November 1953

QUINTON YOUNG
1972–76

Quinton 'Cutty' Young came to Rangers from Coventry City in October 1972, in part exchange for Colin Stein, and had previously been with Ayr United. In fact his origins were in Drongan, a small mining village in Ayrshire. Young was another example of Rangers' long memory concerning players who had played particularly well against them. He had scored a thumping goal on their visit to Somerset Park back in 1969! Cutty settled in quickly as a winger very much in the style that Jock Wallace admired – strong, hard, busy, direct, well able to take care of himself against the most aggressive defenders. If he was no Henderson, no Johnston, still Young was successful at Ibrox, his style much in keeping with the direct philosophy of Wallace. In the end there were differences between these two sparky characters, and Young was given a free transfer in 1976.

Games:	114
Goals:	38
League Championship:	1974–75
Scottish Cup:	1972–73
League Cup:	1975–76
Born:	Drongan, 19 September 1947

GEORGE DONALDSON
1972–74

In 1970, at the age of fifteen, 'Boy' Donaldson was taken on tour to Germany by Willie Waddell, to let him see a brave new world and give him a taste of what the future might offer him. Alas, it held a two-year wait before he reached the 'big' team. George was a strong, stockily built wing-half who did not graduate. He was given a free transfer in April 1974.

Games:	10
Goals:	0
Born:	Edinburgh, 24 November 1954

TOM FORSYTH
1972–82

Dubbed 'Jaws', a nickname which not surprisingly he detested, Tom was one of the most popular players to appear with the club. The nickname came from his style of play, which was uncompromising, and the quality of his tackling, which was fearsome. He was bought from Motherwell in October 1972 for £40,000. Originally a midfield player, he was developed as a centre-half by Jock Wallace, and his qualities of power and accurate and confident passing of the ball brought balance to the Rangers defence and added a strong support element to its attack. With Colin Jackson, he formed a solid core at the centre of a very successful team through the seventies. Tom was a very important player for the club.

He is also famous in Rangers' annals for his first goal. It came in the Scottish Cup Final of 1973, fittingly against Celtic. Forsyth's goal was scored from approximately six inches. A Derek Johnstone header had struck one post and rolled along the goal-line; Forsyth, charging in, could not quite reach the ball. It rebounded from the other post and Forsyth, on the goal-line and off balance, stuck out a foot, managed to make contact, and over the line it went.

Forsyth captained Scotland in but his third international appearance, against Switzerland in 1976, and was a prominent member of the squad in the 1978 World Championship Finals competition. He retired because of injury in March 1982, and became manager of Dunfermline Athletic in the autumn. Having formed a close affinity and friendship with Tommy McLean at Ibrox, Forsyth became his coach and assistant manager at Motherwell in 1985 and proved himself enthusiastic and influential with young players.

Games:	324
Goals:	6
League Championship:	1974–75, 75–76, 77–78
Scottish Cup:	1972–73, 75–76, 77–78, 80–81
League Cup:	1975–76, 77–78
Honours:	22 Scotland caps (21 with Rangers)
Born:	Glasgow, 23 January 1949

JOE MASON
1972–74

Joe Mason was a mature player signed from Morton only a few days after Rangers had been beaten at home by Stenhousemuir (of all people) in a second-round League Cup match. The Rangers team at the time was erratic, all the pieces not yet having fallen into place to make the forceful and successful team of the middle and late seventies. Mason brought intelligence and some style and pattern to the team's play. He was an astute midfield player with a sharp football brain, who became a capable coach to the reserve team during the management of John Greig. He left the club when Greig did, in November 1983.

Games:	19
Goals:	2
Born:	17 August 1940

PHIL BONNYMAN
1972–73

Phil was a left-side midfield player, signed from Hamilton Avondale, who managed only one game with the club – the 1–2 defeat at Ibrox by Stenhousemuir on 4 October 1972 in a League Cup second-round match. He played inside-right that day – rather a bitter souvenir of his season with the club. He was freed and later played with Hamilton Academicals and Carlisle United and became a player–coach with Dunfermline Athletic.

Games:	1
Goals:	0
Born:	Glasgow, 6 February 1954

ALEX O'HARA
1973–77

Alex made his debut for the club at the age of sixteen in a League Cup tie at Falkirk, scoring two goals. He had a very substantial talent for the game, either in midfield or as an inside-forward, and at 5'10" he certainly looked the part. It may have been that a lack of the discipline and dedication which Rangers demand sent him into the lower divisions with Partick Thistle and Morton.

Games:	45
Goals:	10
Born:	Glasgow, 21 October 1956

DOUG HOUSTON
1973–74

Signed at the end of season 1972–73 by Jock Wallace, from Dundee for a fee of £50,000, Doug Houston played full-back or midfield on the left side of the field. He was an experienced player in his late twenties, intelligent, thoughtful, sophisticated and by no means over-physical in action. Injuries inhibited his time at Ibrox, and he never became a regular. He went to Dundee United within a year.

Games:	17
Goals:	0
Born:	Glasgow, 13 April 1943

ERIC MORRIS
1973–79

Eric was an exceptional player as a junior, playing outside-left with Irvine Meadow in the Junior Cup Final when they beat Cambuslang Rangers. He was twenty-three when he reached Ibrox, and never did break into the team on any regular basis. He signed for Ayr United in September 1979.

Games:	11
Goals:	1
Born:	Stranraer, 30 September 1951

JOHNNY HAMILTON
1973–78

Freed by Hibernian, 'Ding-y' Hamilton was snapped up in May 1973. He was a deep-lying inside-forward with a Benburb junior background, and he was very much the play-maker. Pace was probably not his forte, but his passing skills were finely honed and he would keep his outside-right well supplied. He played a prominent role in the League Championship of the treble-winning team of 1975–76 and won a Scottish Cup medal that year. He was freed in the summer of 1978 with Colin Stein despite having won a League Cup medal that season, a fate he had also suffered with Hibernian in 1972–73.

Games:	76
Goals	8
League Championship:	1975–76
Scottish Cup:	1975–76
League Cup	1977–78
Born:	Glasgow, 10 July 1949

TOMMY McLEAN
1971–82

One of the most intelligent and perceptive footballers to play for Rangers, indeed one of the best players produced in Scotland in the past thirty years, Tommy McLean followed a sequence of outstanding outside-rights – Willie Waddell, Alex Scott, Willie Henderson – and in many respects might be considered the greatest of them all. His height of 5'4" belied his ability, which was immense. He was not, like Henderson or Johnston, a dribbler. He was not, like Waddell or Scott, a powerful runner. But he was meticulous in his crossing, primly precise in his passing, the accuracy of his entire game, with either foot, making him a goal-maker supreme and a mainstay of Rangers throughout the decade of the seventies, when his positional sense and distribution were unequalled in Scotland. His long passing, and in particular his crosses, brought goals galore from the men in the centre, specifically Derek Johnstone, Derek Parlane, even Alex Macdonald.

He was signed by Willie Waddell in Copenhagen in 1971, when on international duty, for a fee of £65,000 from the Kilmarnock club. Waddell had earlier signed him as a youngster when he was manager of Kilmarnock. When Tommy came to Ibrox he was already an international player, mature and in his middle twenties; he had already tasted European competition.

McLean retired after the Scottish Cup Final of 1982, becoming coach and assistant manager to John Greig at Ibrox. When Greig left in October 1983, McLean took command of the team, and did it very well until Jock Wallace arrived. He became part-time manager of Morton, then in the summer of 1984 he became manager of Motherwell where he is now a director of the club. His brothers have been prominent in Scottish football management – Jim as managing director of Dundee United, Willie as a former manager of Motherwell.

Games:	449
Goals:	57
League Championship:	1974–75, 75–76, 77–78
Scottish Cup:	1972–73, 75–76, 77–78, 78–79
League Cup:	1975–76, 77–78, 78–79
European Cup Winners' Cup:	1971–72
Honours:	6 Scotland caps (1 with Rangers)
Born:	Larkhall, Lanarkshire, 2 June 1947
Kilmarnock	
League Championship:	1964–65

IAN McDOUGALL
1973–77

A wing-half signed from Pollock Juniors, Ian played quite often without establishing himself in the team. One of his pleasant memories may be a goal scored against Celtic at Parkhead in September 1974, when Rangers won 2–1. He was transferred to Dundee in August 1978 for £15,000.

Games: 37
Goals: 3
League Championship: 1974–75
Born: Baillieston, 14 August 1954

DONALD HUNTER
1973–75

Reserve goalkeeper in the time of McCloy, Kennedy and company, there were few chances for Donald to shine. He was loaned to St Mirren for a spell and went to Dumbarton in 1975.

Games: 4
Shutouts: 2
Born: Dumbarton, 1 April 1955

ALLY SCOTT
1973–76

Scott made an immediate impact with Rangers. Signed from Queen's Park in the summer of 1973, he went straight into the team in the first match of the new season, a League Cup tie against Falkirk – and scored two goals! Repeating that, sustaining that kind of performance, was more than anyone could expect. Alistair Scott was a big fellow, six feet tall, a bustling, all-action, rumbustious striker, a disturber of defences. Articulate and something of an intellectual, his mannerisms and hairstyle (and lack of it) earned him the tag of 'Bamber Gascoigne' in the dressing room. He and Graham Fyfe went to Hibs in exchange for Iain Munro on 7 April 1976. Alistair was subsequently in the insurance business in Glasgow.

Games: 54
Goals: 19
Born: Glasgow, 26 August 1950

DAVID ARMOUR
1974–79

A midfield player signed in 1974 from Shamrock Juveniles, David moved to Ayr United in September 1979.

Games: 4
Goals: 0
Born: 11 April 1953

RICHARD SHARP
1974–75

Brother of Graham, of Everton and Scotland fame, Richard played only one game for Rangers, a League Cup tie against Hibs at Easter Road which was lost 3–1. He was a centre-forward, tall and strong, who left Rangers, left football in fact, for a police career.

Games: 1
Goals: 0
Born: Glasgow, 26 January 1956

MARTIN HENDERSON
1974–78

A tall, rangy centre-forward, Martin was particularly prominent, and a regular scorer, in the treble team of 1975–76. It was the one season of sustained form he enjoyed in the four he spent with the club. Many games that season were won 'single handedly' by decisive Henderson goals. He went to Hibs on loan for three months, then in April 1978 was transferred to Philadelphia Furies for £30,000.

Games: 46
Goals: 14
League Championship: 1975–76
Scottish Cup: 1975–76
Born: Kirkcaldy, 3 May 1956

GORDON BOYD
1975–76

A midfield player, highly talented, Gordon showed quite staggering promise as a schoolboy, so much so that he was being compared to Pelé at that age. He showed the same skills on joining Rangers, but a lack of self-discipline and dedication, and an obvious abhorrence of training, brought his career to a full stop. So highly did Rangers think of him that he was given another chance, around 1980, but the same thing happened. A Barrhead boy, he simply drifted from the football scene.

Games: 1
Goals: 0
Born:: Glasgow, 27 March 1958

STEWART KENNEDY
1973–80

The main contender to the crown of Peter McCloy in the Rangers goal of the seventies was Stewart Kennedy, a Stirling lad who came from Stenhousemuir on 2 April 1973 for a fee of £10,000. Kennedy reached Ibrox by an unusual route. He joined Dunfermline Athletic from his local Camelon Juniors in 1967, was reinstated to junior football with Linlithgow Rose in 1969, then decided to try the senior game again with Stenhousemuir in April 1971. His first match for Rangers was against Falkirk at Brockville on 29 August 1973, in a 5–1 win. The following season, 1974–75, when he was an ever-present, saw Rangers win their first League Championship since 1963–64, and from then until 1978 Kennedy and McCloy exchanged the position, swapping seasons, and effectively sharing the honours.

At 6'1" and 11 stone 5 lb, Kennedy was well equipped for the job. He was a fine athlete, sure in handling with quick reflexes, and made a major contribution to Rangers' Championship win in 1974–75. That season he played five times for Scotland, and seemed settled in the national team until its defence was overrun at Wembley in a disastrous, comprehensive 5–1 defeat by England. Kennedy was never capped again. Many friends of Rangers felt that his unjustified treatment by the Scottish selectors was such that he was never quite the same goalkeeper again. He moved to Forfar Athletic on a free transfer at the end of April 1980 and continued his career there, still playing at the age of forty.

Games:	131
Shutouts:	45
League Championship:	1974–75, 77–78
League Cup:	1975–76, 77–78
Honours:	5 Scotland caps
Born:	Stirling, 31 August 1949

BOBBY McKEAN
1974–78

A product of the junior Blantyre Victoria, Bobby was signed from St Mirren in September 1974 for £60,000. Originally an outside-right, he could play on either side of the team and became a competent midfield player. He was fairly skilful and could go off on mazy dribbles. But he was a purposeful player, a good tackler, strong all round and could score goals. He formed a particularly effective right-wing partnership with Tommy McLean in the Championship of 1974–75. In fact, he was a clear success in his first two seasons at Ibrox, but then inconsistency cost him a regular place, although he remained a useful squad member. He may have been distracted by problems off the field. On 16 March 1978 Bobby McKean was found dead in his car beside his home in Barrhead. He had committed suicide.

Games:	118
Goals:	17
League Championship:	1974–75, 75–76
Scottish Cup:	1975–76
Honours:	1 Scotland cap
Born:	East Kilbride, 15 March 1952

ALLY DAWSON
1975–87

Alistair Dawson joined Rangers as a sixteen-year-old boy in 1975 and was promptly taken on a world tour by manager Jock Wallace. He made his debut in Canada. Alistair was a skilful, cultured full-back who could play on either side. He became the club captain, although he perhaps never quite became the wholly exceptional player everyone expected him to be, possibly because of a serious injury he sustained on a club tour of Canada in 1980 when he fractured his skull. He recovered, of course, and went on to become a poised, neatly balanced central defender, winning his League Cup medal of 1986–87 in that position. He was highly thought of by Jock Stein, the Scotland team manager. Dawson joined Blackburn Rovers for £25,000 in 1987. To date, he is the last Rangers captain to lift the Scottish Cup.

Games:	316
Goals:	9
Scottish Cup:	1978–79, 80–81
League Cup:	1978–79, 83–84, 84–85, 86–87
Honours:	5 Scotland caps
Born:	Johnstone, 25 February 1958

KENNY WATSON (2)
1975–81

Signed from Montrose for £30,000 on 3 August 1975 by Jock Wallace, Kenny was originally a left-side midfield player, but he also played in central defence and as a sweeper. He was rather one-footed, but nevertheless established himself for a spell under John Greig, playing 'out of his skin' in a superb Rangers European Champions Cup win in Eindhoven over PSV. And he had a decisive hand in one of the Rangers goals! That was in March 1979, and was PSV's first defeat at home in any European competition. Kenny moved to Partick Thistle in 1981.

Games:	93
Goals:	6
Scottish Cup:	1977–78, 78–79
Born:	15 December 1951

CHRIS ROBERTSON
1977–80

Brother of John, of Hearts, Newcastle United and Hearts again, Chris is also a striker and was an able goal-scorer in the reserves, but not in the first team. On release he went to Hearts, then to Meadowbank Thistle.

Games:	21
Goals:	3
Born:	Edinburgh, 25 December 1957

JIM STEELE
1976–77

As his name suggests, Jim was a Stalin of a player, a defender with very red hair who came up from Southampton on loan for a month which was littered with bookings. Impossible to play against, Jim came, saw and made many impressions. His loan period was not extended.

Games:	5
Goals:	0
Born:	Edinburgh, 11 March 1950
Southampton	
FA Cup:	1975–76

IAIN MUNRO
1976–78

Alexander Iain Fordyce Munro had a remarkable playing career. It began in that forcing ground for young Glasgow footballers, Drumchapel Amateurs, and took him in turn to St Mirren, Hibernian, Rangers, St Mirren again, Stoke City, Sunderland, Dundee United and back to Hibernian.

Skilled, stylish, cultured, Iain was a left-side midfield player who reached Ibrox from Hibs in April 1976 in exchange for Graham Fyfe and Ally Scott. He was converted into a left-back and in terms of his overall career, this was greatly beneficial to the player – although for no apparent reason, he played a rather limited number of games in his short time with Rangers. His abilities might have been used much more and to better effect. He moved to St Mirren (where he had already been from 1968 to 1973) for £25,000 and in this spell at Love Street was capped seven times for Scotland in 1979 and 1980. In October 1980 he went to Stoke City for £150,000, six times what St Mirren had paid for him, then for the same fee to Sunderland in July 1981. In 1984 he was at Dundee United, in 1985 back at Hibs. His polished skills, with the single defence-splitting pass a speciality, and a high work-rate sustained this long and varied career, which took him into coaching at Dunfermline Athletic. He later became assistant manager to, and then in 1989 joint manager with, Jim Leishman at the Fife club, before ascending to sole managership, under controversial circumstances in July 1990.

Games:	11
Goals:	1
Honours:	7 Scotland caps (none with Rangers)
Born:	Uddingston, 24 August 1951

ROBERT RUSSELL
1977–87

Robert Russell came from Shettleston Juniors in 1977 and made his debut that year in a pre-season game against Nairn County in which he scored a fine goal. This goal was a portent of goals to come, this game the overture to ten marvellous years at Ibrox. Quite simply, Robert Russell was one of the best players Rangers have had since 1970. He had great talent, a stunning first touch on the ball which he used with vision, and he could dribble like an old-timer. He played inside-right or right midfield, and was comparable in style perhaps to the late John White of Blanchflower's famous double team of the early sixties at Tottenham.

If he is remembered for nothing else, it will be for one of the most startling, most audacious, most perfect goals ever scored in European competition. In a second-round European Champions Cup match in October 1978, PSV Eindhoven had come away from Ibrox with a 0–0 draw. In the second-leg match in Holland, PSV scored in just thirty-four seconds! But Rangers, playing with verve and rare discipline, twice equalised, and with three minutes to play and the score 2–2, were under siege by PSV seeking the goal that would take them through. If Rangers held that score, they would go through on the away-goals rule. Yet another PSV attack was headed clear by Derek Johnstone, and the ball picked up by Gordon Smith on the edge of the penalty area. He slanted a pass with his left foot out to Tommy McLean, wide and free on the right wing in his own half. There were two defenders between him and the goalkeeper. McLean shattered these two defenders by clipping a beautiful ball beyond them, and Russell, coming through the centre at speed, had possession. In an instant he was in control and went on calmly to the edge of the penalty area. The goalkeeper, van Engelen, came out and did everything he should have done, did everything right; he came out the correct distance, closed off the angle. Russell could have chipped him or dribbled round him. Instead, he bent his shot round the goalkeeper and into the net. In accuracy, speed and brilliant execution, from Johnstone's head to Russell's shot, it was a stupefying goal. And it brought PSV their first defeat at home in any European match.

After his Rangers decade, Robert went to Motherwell, where he showed the same style and form. Often selected for Scotland, injury each time denied him his cap.

Games:	370
Goals:	46
League Championship:	1977–78
Scottish Cup:	1977–78, 78–79, 80–81
League Cup:	1978–79, 81–82, 83–84, 84–85
Born:	Glasgow, 11 February 1957

BILLY MACKAY
1975–85

Diminutive, red-haired outside-right who made his debut at Pittodrie, August 1977. He had a powerful shot and a tremendous turn of speed, but the presence of Tommy McLean, then David Cooper, denied him a regular place. Sadly, injury led him to retire in 1985, the club giving him a testimonial match against New Zealand. He did come back later to play a few games with Hearts.

Games:	36
Goals:	4
Born:	Glenrothes, 27 October 1960

DEREK STRICKLAND
1977–80

Signed for Rangers in July 1977, he was a skilful inside-forward much in the Derek Ferguson mould. He made his first team debut as a substitute in the John Greig testimonial match of April 1978 (5–0 *v* a Scotland XI). Derek was transferred to Leicester City in part-exchange for Gregor Stevens on 6 September 1979.

Games:	2
Goals:	0

BILLY URQUHART
1978–80

Billy, a Highland lad, was another of John Greig's early signings, on the strength of a pre-season game Rangers had played against his team, Inverness Caledonian, in July 1978 (Rangers won 6–3). Urquhart was a strongly built, enthusiastic type of player who, if he would never win the skill award of any year, could score goals. He played in the European Champions Cup quarter-final tie against Cologne in 1978–79 after having won a League Cup medal earlier that season. He went to Wigan Athletic for £20,000 in November 1980.

Games:	26
Goals:	7
League Cup:	1978–79
Born:	22 November 1956

GEORGE YOUNG
1978–80

A solid, competent, dependable goalkeeper, George was signed from Stirling Albion for £20,000. The presence of Peter McCloy and Stewart Kennedy meant that he was deprived of any chance of competing for a first-team place.

Games:	2
Shutouts:	0
Born:	8 November 1949

GORDON SMITH
1977–80, 1982–83

Bearer of a noble football name, this Gordon Smith would vie with Stuart Munro as Jock Wallace's biggest bargain signing. Gordon came from Kilmarnock in August 1977 for £65,000 and contributed to a very large extent in the transformation of a barren 76–77 into a treble-winning 77–78 for the club, when Rangers played their best football of the seventies. The forward line of McLean, Russell, Johnstone, Smith and Cooper at times ran amok. Johnstone had thirty-seven goals, Smith twenty-six. He had never been known as a goal-scorer with Kilmarnock, but his partnership with Derek Johnstone tore defences apart.

He had arrived at Ibrox as an outside-left, but Wallace made him a deep, left-side midfield player, breaking forward at speed, or alternatively an out-and-out striker. Smith relished it all. He was dark, good-looking, had good pace with a loping stride and a hard right-foot shot. He had pedigree, too – his great-grandfather 'Mattha' Smith had won Scottish Cup medals with Kilmarnock in 1920 and, as captain, in 1929.

Gordon Smith played an important part in Rangers' European Championships and domestic Cup campaigns in 1978–79. He went to Brighton and Hove Albion for a quite astonishing fee of £400,000 in 1980 and, unhappily, will be best remembered for his spell there for a fearful close-range miss in the dying moments of the FA Cup Final of 1983 against Manchester United, seen of course by millions on television.

Gordon was recalled to Rangers in controversial circumstances, on loan, only a matter of days before the League Cup Final of 1982 against Celtic, and put straight into the team. Rangers lost 2–1. It was a gamble by John Greig which did not come off. Gordon later played in Austria and Switzerland, then had his own insurance and financial consultancy business in Glasgow, advising Scottish footballers on investments.

Games:	157
Goals:	51
League Championship:	1977–78
Scottish Cup:	1977–78, 78–79
League Cup:	1977–78, 78–79
Born:	29 December 1954

GREGOR STEVENS
1979–84

Gregor Stevens had what can be described as an interesting career – it was certainly different from that of your average Rangers footballer. As a young player with Motherwell he attracted the attention of many clubs, Celtic and St Etienne among them, but he went to Leicester City for £165,000. He joined Rangers in September 1979 for £150,000 and Derek Strickland, and seemed sure to have a wonderful career chance at Ibrox as a central defender.

Gregor was slim and fiery, went for everything and everybody, and argued with everyone. Off the field he was the perfect family man, living quietly in Torrance. During his five years with Rangers he was sent off five times, booked nineteen times. He was sent off three times in season 1980–81, and his days at the club were surely numbered when, controversially, he was suspended by the SFA for six months in March 1982 following his ordering-off during a friendly(!) with Kilmarnock. He was given a free transfer in May 1984, and later played with Brechin City and Dumbarton. He was ordered off in his debut match with Dumbarton, and, early in the 1989–90 season, with Brechin. Gregor is said to have been sent off twelve times in his career.

Games:	92
Goals:	4
Scottish Cup:	1980–81
League Cup:	1981–82
Born:	Glasgow, 13 January 1955

DAVIE COOPER
1977–89

Clearly one of the most gifted players in the Scottish game, Davie Cooper has also been one of the most enigmatic, inconsistent and irritating, a player whose brilliant mazy dribbles could take him waltzing past bewildered defenders, but at other times lead him into blind alleys and dead ends from which he would have to extract himself. An outside-left, his left foot has been compared to that of Jim Baxter. They operated in different areas of the field, of course, and many observers have felt that he was more effective on the right when coming inside the full-back to favour his left foot in that way.

Cooper was a menacing crosser of a ball, and possessed a thundering shot from dead-ball situations – for example one scored against Jim Leighton from a freekick in the Rangers–Aberdeen League Cup Final of 1987; a decisive goal for Scotland against Australia in a World Cup qualifying match in 1985; and a critical penalty kick against Wales at Cardiff in the same competition in the same year. Many people felt that if Scotland manager Alex Ferguson had made better use of him in the 1986 World Championship finals in Mexico, the team may have qualified for the later stages for the first time. One of his exceptional games was in the 1981 Scottish Cup Final replay when, almost on his own, he tore the Dundee United defence apart.

David was signed from Clydebank in June 1977 for £100,000. Quiet and reserved, in his early years he shunned publicity, and as a printer in Hamilton he turned down numerous transfer offers from English clubs before joining Rangers. When he did, there was much talk of him being indifferent to going to Ibrox and being perfectly happy at Clydebank. The truth is more likely to be that the transfer had been arranged and agreed long before it happened, since Cooper is by way of being a modest 'Blue-nose' This may have been demonstrated when Maurice Johnston arrived at the club in July 1989. In presenting him to the players, it is alleged that Graeme Souness said, 'Here he is, does anyone have anything to say?' Cooper is alleged to have said, 'He shouldn't be here.' True or false, the fact is that one month later Cooper was transferred to Motherwell for £50,000. There he enjoyed a new lease of life, and was called back to the Scotland team by Andy Roxburgh for the deciding World Championship qualifying match in November 1989, against Norway.

Games:	540
Goals:	70
League Championship:	1977–78, 86–87, 88–89
Scottish Cup:	1977–78, 78–79, 80–81
League Cup:	1977–78, 78–79, 81–82, 83–84, 84–85, 86–87, 87–88
Honours:	22 Scotland caps (20 with Rangers)
Born:	Hamilton, 25 February 1956.

ALEX FORSYTH
1978–81

One of John Greig's first signings, Alex came to Ibrox from Manchester United in the first place on a one-season loan arrangement, at the end of which he was signed on a permanent basis. Rangers thus had a mature, vastly experienced and thoroughly able full-back who was mainly held in reserve. He had been on Arsenal's ground staff at the age of fifteen, but homesickness drove him back to Scotland after eight or nine months and he joined Partick Thistle. There he gained his first Scotland cap, and played in the League Cup-winning team of 1971–72, becoming therefore, in the eyes of Thistle fans, immortal. Tommy Docherty, who had first selected him for Scotland, took him to Manchester United in December 1972 for £85,000, and in half a dozen years at Old Trafford Alex became a well-balanced, hard-tackling, stocky defender who could play on either side and get forward into attack, if he perhaps lacked pace in recovery against the faster wingers. He also had a quite thunderous shot. He was given a free transfer in the summer of 1982 and had a season with Motherwell and a season with Hamilton Accies before retiring.

Games:	41
Goals:	5
Honours:	10 Scotland caps (none with Rangers)
Born:	Swinton, Lanarkshire, 5 February 1952
Partick Thistle	
League Cup:	1971–72

GORDON DALZIEL
1976–84

Gordon was a forward – fast, pacy, and with a nose for goals. He was first noted by Rangers fans for a goal he scored after five minutes in a cracking 3–3 draw with Celtic at Parkhead in November 1981. He linked well with John MacDonald in attack, but like MacDonald did not reach full potential with Rangers and became rather a fringe player. He was transferred to Manchester City in 1984, later playing with Partick Thistle and Raith Rovers.

Games:	47
Goals:	11
League Cup:	1981–82
Born:	Motherwell, 16 March 1962

ROBERT CLARK
1980–82

Robert, from Blantyre Victoria, was a tall, slim defender who distributed the ball well and looked like a good player. He never did find a permanent place in the team. Freed, he later played for Motherwell and Kilmarnock.

Games:	1
Goals:	0
Born:	Hamilton, 4 November 1962

IAN REDFORD
1980–86

Rangers set a new record fee between Scottish clubs when they paid Dundee £210,000 for Ian Redford. The date was 22 February 1980, and Ian got in thirteen League matches during the rest of that season. He was a tall, stylish, powerful-running player, good in the air and with a strong shot. An articulate man, Redford was the son of a prosperous farmer in Perthshire. He achieved a certain notoriety with Rangers fans for his last-minute penalty failure against Dundee United in the Scottish Cup Final of 1981. Ian's shot was hard and straight, and goalkeeper McAlpine somehow got his legs to it. But it should be said that it was Redford's dramatic last-minute equaliser against St Johnstone at Perth in the fourth round that kept Rangers alive in that competition. And it also should be said that Redford produced a winner two minutes from the end of the League Cup Final of 1981–82, against Dundee United. He was transferred to Tannadice in August 1985, and he moved on to Ipswich Town.

Games:	247
Goals:	42
Scottish Cup:	1980–81
League Cup:	1981–82, 84–85
Born:	Perth, 5 April 1960

JIM BETT
1980–83

One of the strangest routes ever taken to Ibrox was trodden by Jim Bett, the Aberdeen and Scotland midfield player. A Hamilton boy, he went from schools football there to Airdrieonians by way of being, briefly, an 'associate schoolboy' with Dundee. In May 1978 he was transferred to, of all places, Valur FC of Reykjavik, Iceland, for £1500, and during a short spell there married an Icelandic girl. Bett moved on and up, to SK Lokeren in Belgium where John Greig 'discovered' him and paid £180,000 to bring him to Ibrox in June 1980. Although he had complete success with Rangers, and won Cup medals with them, domestic reasons took him back to Lokeren in the summer of 1983. Two years later Aberdeen persuaded him back to Scotland at a cost of £300,000. With the north-eastern club he has won further medals and established himself firmly as a member of the Scotland team.

Jim Bett was an outstanding Rangers player, a first-class footballer much admired, incidentally, by Graeme Souness. A midfield player, he was two-footed, intelligent, skilful, with a killing first touch on the ball. In a sense he may have been a little before his time at Ibrox, when the team played a more vigorous game than those which came later in the eighties. Like Ray Wilkins, he was not inclined to release the ball until he was sure of its target. In that respect Jim was the strong, safe, conservative type in distribution, preferring the simple pass, the simple option. On arrival at Ibrox he made an immediate impact on the team with the quality and control of his play. He was somehow never wholly accepted by the fans, who recognised him as highly capable but thought him inconsistent.

Games:	152
Goals:	30
Scottish Cup:	1980–81
League Cup:	1981–82
Honours:	26 Scotland caps (2 with Rangers)
Born:	Hamilton, 25 November 1962
Aberdeen:	
Scottish Cup:	1985–86
League Cup:	1989–90

JOHN MacDONALD
1978–86

Yet another of John Greig's earliest signings, John MacDonald was one of the most promising young players in Scotland during the seventies. As a striker he was on the small side (5' 9"), dark, bustling, always in place when the crosses came in, a goal-scorer. He got most of them from around the six-yard range, a scrambler of goals as much as anything, picking up chances, pecking at crumbs. He did it all very well, and was probably most effective playing alongside a big, target centre-forward. In his early years at Ibrox he was a prominent scorer, but his form fell off, in spite of the chances given to him by a succession of managers. He went to Barnsley.

Games:	227
Goals:	78
Scottish Cup:	1980–81
League Cup:	1981–82, 83–84
Born:	Glasgow, 15 April 1961

COLIN MacADAM
1980–85

Colin MacAdam was the first player to feature in a 'tribunal transfer' in Scottish football history. Rangers' notion of his worth in the summer of 1980, when they sought to buy him from Partick Thistle, was £80,000. Thistle were sure he was a £500,000 player. The tribunal priced him at £165,000. Colin forced himself into the record books again by playing for Rangers against Celtic at Parkhead in August 1980 – a game in which Jim Bett scored – in direct opposition to his brother Tom, centre-half for Celtic. He did it more than once, notably three months later in November, when centre-forward Colin scored twice against his brother in a 3–0 Rangers win at Ibrox.

In his first season with the club, Colin scored twenty-two goals. MacAdam was a big (6' 1") powerful lad, versatile and strong in the air, if ball skills and close control were not his strongest suits. Before Partick Thistle he had played at Dumbarton and Motherwell, and it was Bertie Auld at Partick Thistle who converted him from centre-half to centre-forward with a good deal of success. After his bright start at Ibrox, Colin rather languished in the reserves until Jock Wallace revived his career somewhat by moving him back to central defence. As a PE teacher, Colin had always been a part-time player. He was released by Rangers on 30 March 1985.

Games:	99
Goals:	32
League Cup:	1983-84
Born:	Glasgow, 28 August 1951

JIM McINTYRE
1981–82

Jim McIntyre must be rated one of the great disappointments of the early eighties, indeed of this whole period under review. He first came to national notice in the annual Under-15 international against England, when he was quite outstanding. He played briefly with the junior Irvine Meadow and came to Ibrox as a teenager. At 5'7" and sturdily built, he was a super-active wing-half, covering the entire field, and seemed to have the potential of becoming another, say, Billy Bremner. But Jim had a moment of madness by turning out without permission for another, minor, club while a registered Rangers player. He was released. No other senior club came along with an offer, and he went back to Irvine Meadow.

Games:	1
Goals:	0
Born:	Kilwinning, 26 October 1962

KENNY BLACK
1981–84

A left-side full-back or midfield player, Kenny was originally with Rangers on a schoolboy form. He reached the League team in 1981 and in his first two appearances was booked, against Hibs at Easter Road then sent off against Dundee United at Tannadice, thereby making an immediate name of sorts for himself. He was an attacking full-back, hard-tackling although small, very compact, and altogether a rather fearsome, combative player. In December 1983 he and Kenny Lyall were transferred to Motherwell in exchange for goalkeeper Nick Walker. Black later moved to Hearts and, in 1989, to Portsmouth.

Games:	33
Goals:	2
Born:	Stenhousemuir, 29 November 1963

JOHN McCLELLAND
1981–85

John McClelland was the Irish international central defender who had played with Portadown in Ireland, Cardiff City in Wales, and came from Mansfield Town in England to Rangers, just possibly a unique four-country career record. John Greig paid the English club £100,000 for him in May 1981, and he became something of a cornerstone in the Rangers defence, forming a sound partnership with Craig Paterson in the core of the defence in 1982 and 1983, by which time he had become Rangers captain. McClelland was tall at 6' 2" and heavily built, but in spite of that very fast on his feet. Greig took him on a pre-season tour to Sweden in 1981, where he played initially at left-back, and an ankle injury received there dogged his early days with the club. Before joining Rangers he had played left-back and even midfield for Northern Ireland, and during his best days at Ibrox he was certainly one of the best defensive footballers in the UK, conservative in positional play and never a taker of any risks whatsoever. Rangers fans were genuinely sorry to see him go in November 1984, following a dispute over money with manager Wallace. He was smartly transferred to Watford for a record £265,000.

Games:	153
Goals:	8
League Cup:	1983–84, 84–85
Honours:	52 Northern Ireland caps (25 with Rangers)
Born:	Belfast, 7 December 1955

JIM STEWART
1981–84

Circumstances, and perhaps particularly the change of management from John Greig to Jock Wallace in November 1983, meant that James Garven Stewart, the Scottish international goalkeeper, had rather a short career with Rangers. He was signed by Greig on 15 March 1981 for £115,000 from Middlesbrough. Three days later he played against Dundee United when they had one of their very infrequent wins at Ibrox – 4–1 – a rather less than joyous start for any goalkeeper. By the end of the season, however, that score was reversed and Stewart had a Scottish Cup winner's medal in his glove, as Rangers beat Dundee United in the final. Against that same United he won a League Cup Final the following season.

Stewart, a Kilwinning boy, became the regular Kilmarnock goalkeeper, by way of Troon Juniors, when he was but eighteen. He was capped at youth, Under-21 and Under-23 as well as at senior level, and went to Middlesbrough in May 1978 for £110,000. He stood 6'2", built for the job, and was a fine goalkeeper. Some people believed that the word 'fine' was particularly applicable to him and that he was too polite in action to be a real Rangers goalkeeper. He had had to play second best in his later time at Middlesbrough to Jim Platt, the North of Ireland goalkeeper, and of course Peter McCloy was still around at Ibrox.

He was blamed for the loss of critical 'away' goals to Dukla Prague at Ibrox in September 1981, and to Cologne at Ibrox in 1982. The German goal in fact should never have been allowed – it came from a freekick by Allofs, who actually played the ball twice. Stewart's form for Rangers declined. He went to Dumbarton on loan for a spell in 1983–84 and, following a free transfer from Rangers in the summer, moved on to St Mirren as understudy to Campbell Money. He played in the infamous League match, the last of the season in May 1986, when St Mirren lost to Celtic 5–0 at Love Street, a controversial result which allowed Celtic to win the Championship.

Games:	92
Shutouts:	34
Scottish Cup:	1980–81
League Cup:	1981–82
Born:	Kilwinning, 9 March 1954

BILLY DAVIES
1980–86

Signed as a schoolboy – another graduate of Crookston Castle Secondary School – Billy made his debut in Hamilton, Ontario as a substitute in the final of a close-season tournament, the 'Red Leaf Cup', against Ascoli of Italy. Rangers lost 2–0. He was a left-side midfield player, medium height, active, stocky, a perfectly good little player who proved not quite good enough and who was never fully established in the team. He was released when Graeme Souness arrived at Ibrox, went to Sweden briefly, then came back to play with St Mirren. During his time with Rangers, he won Scottish youth honours.

Games:	21
Goals:	2
Born:	Glasgow, 31 May 1964

KENNY LYALL
1981–84

Kenny Lyall, an Edinburgh boy, was a left-side midfield player of very few appearances who was transferred to Motherwell with Kenny Black in exchange for Nicky Walker in December 1983.

Games:	11
Goals:	0
Born:	Edinburgh, 23 March 1963

DOUGLAS ROBERTSON
1981–84

A bustling inside-forward who forced his way into the first team for a few matches in 1981 but could not sustain his place, Dougie had something of a weight problem which hindered him. He went to Morton in 1984 for a small fee.

Games:	8
Goals:	0
Born:	Torphichen, 15 March 1963

CRAIG PATERSON
1982–87

A club record fee of £225,000 was paid for Craig Paterson in July 1982 when John Greig bought him from Hibs, but the transfer in a sense turned out to be one of the most disappointing of his managerial career. Craig, son of John Paterson, centre-half in the Hibs team of the late fifties and early sixties had shown immense promise and ability at Easter Road, but injuries dogged his time at Ibrox. Rangers were so anxious to have him signed for a pre-season tournament in Lille that they did not insist on a medical examination before the transfer. Paterson marked his debut in the tournament by scoring the winning goal in the semi-final against St Etienne in a penalty shoot-out. Rangers lost the final to SK Lokeren.

Craig quickly established himself in the Rangers team, forming a very successful central defence partnership with John McClelland. He became captain after McClelland left the club, leading the team to success in the League Cup of 1984–85. His greatest strength was in the air, and he was a ball-player rather than a plain stopper. Injuries and intermittent lapses in form prevented him from being the player he should have been, from fulfilling all his talents. Such was his ability that he should have been, for example, a Scotland international player. Drifting around the fringes of the team, he was sold to Motherwell by Graeme Souness early in his Ibrox regime.

Games:	130
Goals:	12
League Cup:	1983–84, 84–85
Born:	South Queensferry, 2 October 1959

ROBERT PRYTZ
1982–85

A Swedish international signed from Malmö for £100,000, Robert was a seasoned player who had played in the European Champions Cup Final which Malmö lost to Nottingham Forest in Munich in 1979. He was a central or left-sided midfield player. Prytz was strong and stocky, used the ball well and had a terrific finishing shot. He was popular with the players, but perhaps not so with the crowd – they thought he gave less than 100 per cent effort. Perhaps the direct Rangers style was none too compatible with his continental thinking on the game and how it should be played. He scored the winning goal at Pittodrie in a League match in September 1982 to give Rangers their first win there in six years. Robert went to IFK Goteborg for £130,000, and went on to play for Bayern Leverkusen in Germany. More recently he was with Verona in Italy.

Games :	118
Goals:	20
League Cup:	1984–85
Honours:	56 Sweden caps (10 with Rangers) (to end 1989)
Born:	Malmö, 12 January 1960

DAVE McPHERSON
1981–87

Yet another graduate of that football academy, Crookston Castle Secondary School, only a few miles from Ibrox on Glasgow's south side, this giant (6' 3") joined the club as a schoolboy who proved able to play full-back, centre-half or central defender. Commanding in the air, naturally, David was rather untidy and no thoroughbred in movement with the ball at his feet, but was a very competent defender not afraid to make surging runs forward. He made an impressive attacking gambit for Rangers when he went forward for set pieces, and proved very difficult for opposing defences to counter. In 1984 and 1985 he was recognised with Under-21 selection for Scotland. Rangers fans had taken to him – they saw McPherson as a potential club captain, perhaps a latter-day George Young, and a player who gave every match his total endeavour.

It may have been that the arrival of such as Terry Butcher and Graham Roberts under the Souness management made David expendable. Another school of thought has it that Graeme Souness could not forgive him for a mistake in the Scottish Cup-tie of January 1987, which led to Hamilton's winning goal. A long ball from the Accies defence which he failed to control let Adrian Sproat steal possession from him and go on to score the only goal of the match, and Rangers were out of the Cup. The goal brought to an end Chris Woods' British record run of eleven games without conceding a goal. McPherson was transferred to Hearts in the summer for a fee in excess of £300,000. He has been successful with the Edinburgh club, becoming captain of the team and winning his first full Scotland caps.

Games:	222
Goals:	26
League Championship:	1986–87
League Cup:	1983–84, 84–85
Honours:	7 Scotland caps (none with Rangers)
Born:	Paisley, 28 January 1964

ANDY BRUCE
1981–86

Andy was a Scottish Youth international goalkeeper who made a limited number of appearances because of the presence of Peter McCloy and Jim Stewart. He was a perfectly capable goalkeeper, released by Graeme Souness. He went to Hearts, where he was yet again an understudy.

Games:	2
Shutouts:	0
Born:	Edinburgh, 9 August 1964

ANDY KENNEDY
1982–84

Signed from youth football, Andy Kennedy was a striker, very, very fast, in the mould of an Ian Rush, but of course not remotely as good. He was brought into the team by John Greig, and with contemporaries such as Billy Davies and Kenny Black, it seemed that the Rangers youth policy was succeeding. After a lively start, Andy could not maintain his momentum and when Jock Wallace arrived, he lost his place, never to retain it. Released by Wallace, he went to Birmingham City, then to Blackburn Rovers, where he has been perfectly successful.

Games:	20
Goals:	4
Born:	Stirling, 8 October, 1964

DAVE MITCHELL
1983–85

Defenders always knew when Dave Mitchell was around – Dave made sure of that. A six-foot centre-forward hustler from Australia, Mitchell paid his own expenses to Scotland for trials with Rangers and was signed by Greig. He made himself a regular first-team player, and was rather surprisingly transferred by Wallace. He went back to Australia, played against Scotland in the World Championships qualifying tournament of 1986, and played in Germany's Bundesliga with Eintracht Frankfurt.

Games:	45
Goals:	14
Honours:	Australian Internationalist since leaving Rangers
Born:	Glasgow, 13 June 1962

SANDY CLARK
1983–85

If the traditional concept of the 'old-fashioned' centre-forward is one of a strong man, full of running, taking and giving knocks, often injured but spurning the injuries, challenging for everything, active with the elbows, and so on, Sandy Clark was the vintage example. He was, of course, much more than that. Sandy was forceful in the air, courageous in the penalty area, but he could work well and closely with inside-forwards and keep a forward line moving nicely. He played originally with his home-town team, Airdrieonians, then went to West Ham United, from whom Rangers bought him on 17 March 1983 for £160,000. Sandy had been a long-time Rangers supporter, and it had always been an ambition to play for the club. The return to Ibrox of Jock Wallace seemed to restrict Sandy – Wallace appeared to prefer such other forwards as McCoist, Iain Ferguson and David Mitchell. Clark was transferred to Hearts for £40,000 in October 1984, where he played successfully until late 1989 when he joined Partick Thistle as player–manager before going back to Hearts to coach in 1990.

Games:	62
Goals:	21
League Cup:	1983–84
Born:	Airdrie, 28 October 1956

DAVE McKINNON
1982–86

In one of John Greig's surprise transfer deals, McKinnon was signed from Partick Thistle for £30,000 in May 1982. Dave was a red-haired, wholehearted full-back who had pace and was addicted to storming forward to use a powerful shot. He was not a highly cultured player and Rangers fans failed to comprehend this signing – McKinnon had previously been with Arsenal, Dundee and Partick Thistle, so what, they asked, could he do for Rangers? He was given a free transfer by Graeme Souness and moved on to Airdrie.

Games:	141
Goals:	3
Born:	Glasgow, 23 May 1956

JIMMY NICHOLL
1983–84, 1986–89

A seasoned player of high quality, as a career with Manchester United, Sunderland and West Bromwich Albion and more than seventy caps for Northern Ireland confirms, Jimmy joined Rangers originally on loan from Toronto Metro Croatia. A cheerful, outgoing Ulsterman, he was much respected by Rangers fans. Second time around at Ibrox, Graeme Souness brought him from West Bromwich Albion, exchanging Bobby Williamson in the deal in August 1986, and he became a defensive cornerstone in the first Souness team, before the advent of Gary Stevens. Nicholl was technically very sound, experienced and mature and was a useful, valuable and classy player for Rangers. Whilst at Ibrox he coached the second team, and Souness wanted him to stay and develop as a coach. Nicholl felt that he could play on in Premier Division football for a little longer, and he went to Dunfermline Athletic in 1989.

Games:	106
Goals:	0
League Championship:	1986–87
League Cup:	1983–84, 86–87, 87–88
Honours:	73 Northern Ireland caps (4 with Rangers)
Born:	Toronto, Canada, 28 December 1956
Manchester United FA Cup:	1976–77

BOBBY WILLIAMSON
1983–87

A strong, knock 'em down type of centre-forward who could score spectacular goals, Bobby was signed by Jock Wallace from Clydebank for £100,000 in December 1983. On the club's world tour of 1984 he suffered a severe leg break, an injury which kept him out of football for the best part of a year. He was transferred to West Bromwich Albion in August 1986, in exchange for Jimmy Nicholl.

Games: 52
Goals: 20
Born: Glasgow, 13 August 1961

ERIC FERGUSON
1983–86

Many friends of Rangers felt that Eric, a tall, loose-limbed centre-forward, was worth a more extended run in the team than he had. He scored many goals in the reserves. Released in 1986, he went to Dunfermline Athletic.

Games: 13
Goals: 1
Born: Fife, 12 February 1965

NICKY WALKER
1984–89

Jock Wallace, lately the Motherwell manager, swapped Kenny Black, Kenny Lyall and cash, in a deal reckoned to be worth £100,000, to bring his erstwhile goalkeeper Nicky Walker to join him at Ibrox a month or so after he was appointed Rangers manager for a second time. Walker, a native of Elgin and scion of the Walker shortbread family, had his first match at Easter Road on 27 December 1983, when Rangers beat Hibs 2–0. Like Kennedy and Stewart before him, he found himself disputing with Peter McCloy for the position, but season 1985–86 was a particularly successful one for him. He missed only a couple of matches in a season which was completely barren for a team of appalling inconsistency, so much so that after Rangers lost a rather prestigious home friendly with Tottenham Hotspur (a club that has caused them trouble down the years) by 2–0, Jock Wallace departed from the club and Graeme Souness arrived from Sampdoria as his successor in April 1986.

The expensive signing of Chris Woods in the summer of that year, at the same time as Peter McCloy was signing a new two-year contract, meant that Walker went into reserve, although many fans were prepared to say that he should have been the preferred goalkeeper when Woods seemed to be suffering various crises of confidence. Nicky Walker was a competent goalkeeper, and something of a heroic one in the League Cup Final of 1987–88 against Aberdeen, when he replaced the suspended Chris Woods although he was not really fit. Under freedom of contract Walker signed for Hearts in 1989, inexplicably since he became a reserve yet again, this time to Henry Smith.

Games: 95
Shutouts: 37
League Cup: 1987–88
Born: Aberdeen, 29 September 1962

SCOTT FRASER
1983–85

A full-back introduced by Jock Wallace in January 1984 in a home match against Aberdeen, Scott never became a regular choice and was freed in May 1985.

Games:	10
Goals:	0
Born:	Edinburgh, 28 April 1963

STUART MUNRO
1984–

A survivor of the Souness revolution at Ibrox, indeed one of the great unsung heroes of the Souness era of Terry Butcher and Maurice Johnston and the like, Stuart Munro in fact has been much more than just a low-profile survivor. He was signed from Alloa in February 1984 by Jock Wallace for £25,000, now seen to be ridiculously cheap at the price. A left-sided player, he has won over an Ibrox crowd which initially gave him a rough ride. He has seen off all contenders for his left-back position, including such players as Jan Bartram of Denmark and Jimmy Phillips of Bolton Wanderers. Stuart is fast, very quick in recovery, and above all beautifully balanced, like a latter-day Sammy Cox. He relates instinctively to central defenders such as Butcher and Richard Gough, works smoothly with the midfield players and can break forward with enthusiasm and at speed. All told, Munro is a highly competent, well-rounded footballer.

Games:	213
Goals:	3
League Championship:	1986–87, 88–89, 89–90
League Cup:	1986–87, 87–88
Born:	Falkirk, 15 September 1962

ROBERT FLECK
1983–88

Glasgow born and bred, Robert Fleck was a product of the 'system', both of Rangers and of Scotland. Like Derek Ferguson, Hugh Burns and Iain Durrant, Robert took the route through youth teams and Under-21 selections and emerged as a fast, pacy, brave striker with stunning acceleration, and as a regular and reliable goal-scorer. Although only 5'6" tall, he was a powerful runner and finisher. He was the ideal foil to Alistair McCoist (according to McCoist), and they formed a potent strike force, particularly in the Championship of 1986–7. Financial differences, it was believed, led to Fleck making a transfer request, which was certainly not welcomed by Rangers, but in December 1987 he went to Norwich City for £560,000. His going left Rangers woefully short of striking force that season, and may have cost them their chance of advancement in the European Champions Cup. Fleck's talents blossomed in the English First Division, where he scored regularly for the Canaries.

Games:	104
Goals:	34
League Championship:	1986–87
League Cup:	1986–87, 87–88
Honours:	3 Scotland caps (none with Rangers)
Born:	Glasgow, 11 August 1965

DEREK FERGUSON
1982–90

A midfield player who has represented Scotland at youth, Under-2l and senior international level, Derek Ferguson was seen by many friends of Rangers to have the potential to become as good as Paul McStay in the Celtic midfield. Injuries, misdemeanours and other problems off the field have hindered his progress. He was able to contribute little to the Rangers team in season 1989–90, and in midwinter, when the possibility of his transfer arose, it was clear that the Rangers management had lost patience with the player. The Graeme Souness observation was ominous – he said, 'We've been paying him good money for no return in the past couple of years.' Ferguson was loaned to Dundee early in 1990. He was tranferred to Hearts in July 1990 for £750,000.

Games:	145
Goals:	9
League Championship:	1986–87, 88–89
League Cup:	1986–87, 87–88
Honours:	2 Scotland caps
Born:	Glasgow, 31 July 1967

IAIN FERGUSON
1984–86

Iain arrived at Ibrox in May 1984 from Dundee, under freedom of contract and for a 'tribunal' fee of £200,000. He had outstanding ability and was a scorer of thrilling goals, but a certain lack of discipline and commitment meant that he never became another Kenny Dalglish, whereas at one time that had looked entirely possible. He was a reasonably successful signing for Rangers, but perhaps a strict code of discipline was not for him.

Scored the only goal in the League Cup Final of 1984–85 (v Dundee United) and was noted for vital counter in Europe.

Games:	46
Goals:	11
League Cup:	1984–85
Born:	Newarthill, 4 August 1962

CAMMY FRASER
1984–87

HUGH BURNS
1983–87

Like Iain Ferguson, Cameron Fraser was a 'tribunal' transfer from Dundee, only two months later, for a fee set at £165,000. He was a midfield player, strong, stylish, competent but also hard, and he had his problems with referees. He was one of the few players who have appeared in all three major Scottish derby matches – Glasgow, Edinburgh and Dundee. Cammy was a fairly important member of the first Graeme Souness side at Ibrox in League and League Cup, but was forced to retire at the end of the 1986–87 season because of injury. He did make something of a comeback, and played some games with Raith Rovers.

Games:	74
Goals:	9
League Cup:	1984–85, 86–87
Born:	Dundee, 22 July 1957

Hugh Burns, a lively, attacking right-back, broke through into the team during the second Jock Wallace regime. He had been capped at youth and Under-21 levels and was popular with the Rangers crowd because of his exciting forward runs. Under Graeme Souness he lost his place in the team, and following a difference of opinion he was transferred to Hearts. Hugh subsequently joined Dunfermline Athletic, then Fulham.

Games:	63
Goals:	4
League Cup:	1983–84
Born:	Lanark, 13 December 1965

ALISTAIR McCOIST
1983–

The extrovert kid from East Kilbride is one of the most bubbling personalities that Rangers have ever had, and also one of the club's greatest goal-scorers, certainly the finest Rangers have had over the past fifty years. As a result, he is now worshipped by the Rangers legions. 'Twas not ever thus. Alistair signed for Rangers only at the third time of asking. As a schoolboy, he said no to a John Greig approach, and signed for St Johnstone instead on 1 December 1978, aged sixteen. He made his debut for them on 7 April 1979 and had three more games in succession at the end of that season. In season 1980–81 he snapped up twenty-three goals for the Saints, and a flock of clubs were in pursuit of him, Rangers included – and thereby hangs a tale. The story goes that McCoist and a St Johnstone director were at Ibrox, discussing his transfer, in August 1981. There was a telephone call for the St Johnstone director, who left the discussions to take the call. It was from Sunderland, offering £100,000 more than Rangers were suggesting. So McCoist, still only eighteen years old, went to Sunderland for the massive amount for such a young player of £400,000. Thus Rangers had been spurned twice.

His period at Sunderland, in a team that was always struggling, was not a success and in June 1983 Alistair met John Greig and his assistant manager, Tommy McLean, in a Carlisle hotel and signed, at last, for Rangers. The fee was £185,000. Alistair was not welcomed rapturously by the Rangers fans. They were well aware of his history and rather questioned his commitment to a club he had twice rejected. His first two seasons at Ibrox were quite difficult and at one point manager Wallace suggested he should leave, saying he could arrange a transfer back to Sunderland. But McCoist was determined and persisted with Rangers, forcing himself into the team for the latter part of season 84–85, and all of 85–86. At the same time he forced himself into the full Scotland international team, with a first cap in April 1986, against Holland. Since then he has become overwhelmingly popular with the fans, because of his play and personality alike. Alistair is lively, extrovert and articulate, funny and friendly and brilliant at handling media. One can well imagine him making a career in television in the future.

As a striker he is balanced on both sides, sharp, menacing, as brave as can be in going into the tightest of situations and space and taking lots of the knocks and injuries without complaint or retaliation. At 5' 10" he is not particularly excellent in the air, but he does challenge the tallest defenders. Above all, he has the greatest of centre-forward qualities – the art of snapping up the slenderest of chances, of making a good chance out of a half-chance. No footballer has ever enjoyed being a superstar more than Alistair McCoist. No centre-forward has ever enjoyed scoring goals more than Alistair McCoist. In season 1989–90, he set several records; first, the highest number of Premier League goals, his 133 passing Frank McGarvie's 127; he set a Rangers' post-war record with his 133, passing Derek Johnstone's 131, and he scored Rangers' 7000th League goal, against Motherwell at Ibrox on 9 December 1989, in a 3–0 win. His reaction to scoring is liable to be, in his own word, 'demented'. He has an excellent touch and marvellous mobility, some of the qualities of the great Kenny Dalglish in the penalty area, and has formed a successful striking partnership with Maurice Johnston. He has been an expert penalty-taker, probably Rangers' best since Alex Miller. Above all else, it is the obvious joy with which he plays the old game that makes Alistair McCoist one of the most attractive footballers Scotland has seen.

Games:	307
Goals:	181
League Championship:	1986–87, 88–89, 89–90
League Cup:	1983–84, 84–85, 86–87, 87–88, 88–89
Honours:	26 Scotland caps
Born:	Bellshill, 24 September 1962

KEVIN McMINN
1984–87

IAIN DURRANT
1984–

Kevin 'Ted' McMinn would have to be considered an odd, almost comic figure in the Scottish game. A tall, haphazard winger, he would take off on runs without the opposition – or his team-mates for that matter – having the slightest notion of what he had in mind. Nicknamed the 'Tin Man', no doubt because of an apparent lack of physical coordination, Ted could nevertheless score spectacular, sometimes preposterous, goals. He had pace, power and stamina, and his wing play, combined with that of David Cooper, however different, was of major importance in Rangers' League Cup win of 1986–87.

Ted had been bought by Jock Wallace from Queen of the South in October 1984 for £100,000, and he may not have cared much for the Graeme Souness discipline. On the other hand, Souness may not have cared for the McMinn unorthodoxy. He was transferred to Seville for a reunion with his former manager, Wallace, and when he left Seville, McMinn came back to the UK and joined Derby County.

Games: 75
Goals: 5
League Championship: 1986–87
League Cup: 1986–87
Born: Castle Douglas, 28 September 1962

An outstanding left-side midfield player, Iain is a local boy from Govan who joined Rangers as a schoolboy and has come through the club's coaching and training system. He has played for Scotland at youth, Under-18, Under-21 and full international levels. Durrant was a player of high quality, an exciting, quick player with the confidence to run at defenders. He could play, and did, as a forward, but was seen as a player who would balance the Scotland midfield of the future with Paul McStay of Celtic. He suffered an appalling tackle by Neil Simpson of Aberdeen in October 1988; his right knee was virtually shattered and demanded much surgery. He did not play again that season, nor at all in 1989, and the injury may have compromised his career completely.

Games: 160
Goals: 29
League Championship: 1986–87
League Cup: 1986–87, 87–88
Honours: 3 Scotland caps
Born: Glasgow, 19 October 1966

DAVID MACFARLANE
1984–89

A fringe player who played several positions in defence, and who was in the League Cup-winning team of 1986–87, David, 6'2" tall and a youth international, never found a regular place in the team. He was transferred to Kilmarnock in 1989 for £100,000, an exceptional piece of business by Graeme Souness.

Games:	9
Goals:	0
League Cup:	1986–87
Born:	Irvine, 16 January 1967

STUART BEATTIE
1985–87

A youth international centre-half from Ayrshire, Stuart showed much promise as a young player, but his chance in that position surely went with the arrival of Terry Butcher. He was signed from Ardeer Rec. BC, and went to Doncaster Rovers.

Games:	5
Goals:	0
Born:	Stevenston, 10 July 1967

COLIN MILLER
1985–87

Scots-born Colin, a left-side full-back or wing-half, signed in July 1985 from Toronto Blizzard. He played for Canada in the 1986 World Championship qualifying tournament. He was very fast, but rather slightly built, and was released by Graeme Souness, subsequently playing for Doncaster Rovers, Hamilton Steelers (Canada) and Hamilton Academicals.

Games:	3
Goals:	0
Honours:	7 Canada caps
	(2 while with Rangers)
Born:	Lanark, 4 October 1964

DOUGLAS BELL
1985–87

Signed from Aberdeen for £125,000 in May 1985, Dougie Bell had been a very important member of the Aberdeen European Cup Winners' Cup team of 1983, although he did not play in the final. As a ball-winning midfield player with good skills, he was an important squad player at Ibrox in 1986–87, but he may not have been consistent enough for manager Souness. He went on to play variously at St Mirren, Hibs, Shrewsbury Town and Hull City.

Games:	44
Goals:	1
Born:	Paisley, 5 September 1959

Aberdeen	
European Super Cup:	1983–84
League Championship:	1983–84, 84–85
Scottish Cup:	1981–82, 83–84

COLIN WEST
1986–87

SCOTT NISBET
1985–

Graeme Souness's first major signing, Colin was bought from Watford on 15 May 1986 for £200,000. Big and strong, awkward and none too mobile albeit powerful in the air, a combination of injury and the emergence of the McCoist–Fleck striking partnership limited Colin's achievement at Ibrox, and he went back south after one year.

Games:	15
Goals:	3
Born:	Wallsend, 13 November 1962

A versatile player from Edinburgh, Scott can play full-back, centre-half, sweeper, even centre-forward. He turned down a chance to go to Dundee for £300,000 early in season 1989–90, then was the subject of an approach in December 1989, for the same amount, from Blackburn Rovers.

Games:	56
Goals:	2
Born:	Edinburgh, 30 January 1968

CHRIS WOODS
1986–

One of the earliest of a stream of expensive purchases by Graeme Souness in what has become known as the 'Souness era', Chris Woods joined Rangers in June 1986 from Norwich City for £600,000, and in his very first season at Ibrox demonstrated that he was a goalkeeper of the highest class. Already an England international and World Cup player, he had understudied Peter Shilton, whom he was expected to succeed as the regular England goalkeeper, at Nottingham Forest. Indeed, he had won an English League Cup medal with Forest, and had also played for Queen's Park Rangers and Norwich City. In the Championship season of 1986–87, his first with Rangers, he made many dramatic and vital saves and set a British record of successive games without conceding a goal, this run brought to an end by the painful home defeat from Hamilton Accies by one solitary goal in the first-round Scottish Cup tie at Ibrox in January 1987. Tall, blond, with blue eyes, and splendidly athletic, Chris looked as an English goalkeeper should look.

In 1988–89 he was stricken by an uncommon and persistent virus which seriously affected his vision and balance, so much so that he missed most of that season. Then in season 1989–90, in the opening game against St Mirren, he damaged his right shoulder, which cost him more appearances. His manager, not unnaturally since he had paid a small fortune for him, is convinced that Chris is the best goalkeeper in British football. Others have said that his one shortcoming is that he does not defend himself rigorously enough in resisting strong challenges in the air – and Rangers goalkeepers are liable to suffer more of these strong challenges than any others. Given freedom from injury, Woods could be a defensive bastion for Rangers for many years.

Games:	181
Shutouts:	91
League Championship:	1986–87, 88–89, 89–90
League Cup:	1986–87, 88–89
Honours:	16 England caps
	(12 with Rangers)
Born:	Boston, Lincs,
	14 November 1959
Nottingham Forest	
Football League Cup:	1977–78
Norwich City	
Football League Cup:	1984–85

TERRY BUTCHER
1986–

One of the most famous and respected figures in world football, Terry Butcher has captained the team and shown inspirational leadership qualities throughout the Souness era, and is probably the most calculated signing Graeme has made. He came from Ipswich Town in August 1986 for £725,000. The Butcher signing, and the price, coming so closely behind that of Chris Woods, was a clear declaration to the Rangers public and to Scottish football that there was fresh thinking in the Rangers boardroom and on the part of management, and that the club was preparing to challenge the best teams in Europe and to meet them on level terms. As deputy captain of England – he had led his country more than once in the absence of Bryan Robson – Butcher was a seasoned international and World Cup player, a giant of 6' 4'" who dominated the team and the entire field. Over the four years since he joined the club Butcher has been the core of the team, all the other players relating to him in action, all revolving round him. With a pleasant off-field personality at ease with the media, he has been a great ambassador for the club.

As a centre-half, or more accurately a left-side central defender, he has formed an almost invincible central unit in defence with Richard Gough. As one would expect, he has been almost unchallengeable in the air in defence, while in his advances into opposition space for corner kicks and free kicks, his height and sheer size have been enormously difficult to contain.

A broken-leg injury in 1987–88 cost him half of the season, and very probably Rangers' Championship chance. The consequences of his loss to England in the European Championships of 1988 can only be guessed at, and he was a cornerstone in their planning for the 1990 World Championship Finals. In his dedication to the team and hunger for victory, Butcher could be compared to the great John Greig. He plays every one of the ninety minutes, and beyond, and cares passionately for success – so much so that it has been noted that he is sometimes crotchety in his protests to referees. He captained England in the 1990 World Cup semi-final tie against West Germany.

Games:	167
Goals:	10
League Championship:	1986–87, 88–89, 89–90
League Cup:	1986–87, 88–89
Honours:	77 England caps (32 with Rangers)
Born:	Singapore, 28 December 1958
Ipswich Town	
UEFA Cup:	1980–81

GRAEME SOUNESS
1986–

In the past ten years, possibly in the past twenty years, Scotland has produced only two players who beyond any reasonable doubt can be described as truly world-class footballers. They are Kenneth Mathieson Dalglish and Graeme James Souness, contemporaries at Liverpool. Both men have had dazzling careers in the game, and in the eighties both men have made dazzling starts to managerial careers with Liverpool and Rangers respectively, by winning Championship and Cup doubles in their very first season.

Graeme Souness was a Tottenham Hotspur apprentice player in April 1969, aged sixteen, and a full professional at seventeen. He was a schoolboy and youth international as a midfield player. Homesickness and strong competition for selection at Spurs thwarted him, and he moved to Middlesbrough in January 1973 for £30,000. His next move was to Liverpool for £352,000, then a record between English clubs, in January 1978, and at Anfield he had a golden career – three European Championship victories, five English Championships, four English League Cups. During this glittering career were three World Cup competitions, and captaincy of his country.

Souness was a brilliant player – a controller of the middle of the field, a player who could set the pace, rhythm and tactics of his team. He was not noted particularly for pace, or heading ability, but seldom needed either. He was the master of the pass, and especially the long pass, and had a fulminating shot from outside the penalty area when backing up his forward players. Highly talented, he was also a hard player, giving best to no one on the field or, it seems, in his later life, off the field. In World Cup matches in Iceland, and at Hampden against Wales, he was fortunate to stay on the field. In his very first match for Rangers, as player–manager, against Hibs at Easter Road, he was not so fortunate – he was ordered off for blatantly kicking George McCluskey, the Hibs forward. And in his treatment of such players as David McPherson, Graham Roberts and Davie Cooper off the field, as manager, he seemed quite ruthless.

As a ball-winner and play-maker combined, perhaps his most important single game was the European Champions Cup Final of 1984, when Liverpool beat AS Roma on penalties after a 1–1 draw in extra time. Souness so stamped himself on that match that Sampdoria promptly bought him, and he spent two successful and educational years in Italian football.

Although remaining registered as a player at the end of the eighties, Graeme's playing career was effectively over in 1990. He was then in his late thirties.

Games:	73
Goals:	5
League Championship:	1986–87
Honours:	54 Scotland caps (2 with Rangers)
Born:	Edinburgh, 6 May 1953

Middlesbrough	
Football League:	2nd Division Championship 1973–74

Liverpool	
European Champions Cup:	1977–78, 80–81, 83–84
Football League Championship:	1978–79, 79–80, 81–82, 82–83, 83–84
Football League Cup:	1980–81, 81–82, 82–83, 83–84

GRAHAM ROBERTS
1986–88

Graham Roberts came to Rangers from Tottenham Hotspur in December 1986 for £450,000 with the reputation of being a very hard man, a kicker, a fouler. Paradoxically, he was sent off only once in competitive fixtures during his time with the club, in circumstances which Rangers people, naturally, considered amounted to dreadful refereeing decisions. Roberts was certainly a passionate player, the ultimate competitor who would tackle through anything, simply remove people from his path, to get to the ball. He came to Ibrox as a seasoned player – he had helped Spurs to a UEFA Cup win over Anderlecht in 1984 – and fell easily into a successful partnership with Terry Butcher in central defence.

He was a very important player in the Rangers Championship campaign of 1986–87, and captained the League Cup-winning team of the next season. Indeed, he was captain of Rangers throughout Terry Butcher's absence with his broken-leg injury, and was an inspirational player in never knowing when he was beaten. He could also be a ball-winning midfield player, and even a goal-scorer in forcing things home powerfully, perhaps ruthlessly (at 5' 11" and 13 stone) at close range in opposing penalty areas.

His end came dramatically following a 1–0 defeat by Aberdeen, when Roberts felt unfairly accused of having caused the loss of the goal, and of the match. Hard words were exchanged between him and manager Souness, and Roberts played no more for Rangers. He was transferred to Chelsea in time for the new season of 1988–89, for £475,000.

Games:	69
Goals:	3
League Championship:	1986–87
League Cup:	1987–88
Honours:	6 England caps
	(none with Rangers)
Born:	Southampton, 3 July 1959.

Tottenham Hotspur
FA Cup:	1980–81, 81–82
UEFA Cup:	1983–84

AVI COHEN
1987–89

An Israeli international and a contemporary of Graeme Souness at Liverpool, Avi was a central defender or full-back, and a player of style and quality, a solid defender. He came from Maccabi Tel Aviv for £100,000 in the summer of 1987, and his talents gave the Rangers defence a bit of polish, and classy cover. No doubt Souness used him until he could recruit younger players. Cohen's availability was restricted by international calls from Israel for World Cup and Olympic matches, and many Rangers people felt that he could have made a major contribution to the European Champions Cup campaign of 1987–88. The lack of his poise in Bucharest through injury, for example, was a fatal blow. He went back to Israel in 1989, and later played in France.

Games:	12
Goals:	0
League Cup:	1987–88
Honours:	4 Israel caps
	(while with Rangers)
Born:	Cairo, 14 November 1956

NEIL WOODS
1986–88

Neil was a young striker, bought from Doncaster Rovers for £100,000. He was transferred to Ipswich Town in 1988.

Games:	3
Goals:	0
Born:	York, 30 July 1966

DAVID KIRKWOOD
1986–89

Davie came from East Fife as a midfield player in 1987 for £30,000. Initially he showed outstanding promise, but. . . . He was transferred to Hearts.

Games:	10
Goals:	0
Born:	St Andrews, 27 August 1967

JIMMY PHILLIPS
1986–89

A full-back or central defender bought from Bolton Wanderers for £75,000, Jimmy was a very useful player indeed who challenged for Stuart Munro's left-back position. He was transferred to Oxford United in 1989 for £150,000.

Games	33
Goals:	0
Born:	Bolton, 8 February 1966

RICHARD GOUGH
1987–

Richard was born in Stockholm (his mother was Swedish) but spent his early years in South Africa. His father, a Govan man who had played for Charlton Athletic in the sixties, was in business in South Africa, although remaining a Rangers fan, and the young man was sent over in 1980 to play a trial for Rangers, against a Queen's Park team, at Lesser Hampden. Rangers have since been criticised for not having signed him then, but the truth was that he played poorly, and on that evidence didn't deserve to be signed. However, he also played a trial for Dundee United, who liked what they saw and signed him. At one point he 'defected' from Dundee and went back to South Africa, perhaps because of homesickness. He returned, rather reluctantly, to become a fine player and an international with the Tannadice club. Rangers tried to sign him, offering £500,000 in 1986, but the United manager, Jim McLean, refused to sell him to a Scottish club and Gough went to Tottenham Hotspur in August of that year for £750,000. He was very successful in London, quickly becoming Spurs' captain. In December 1987 Rangers at last got their man. Graeme Souness paid a staggering £1,100,000 – a clear indication of the manager's opinion of the player.

Richard is probably the one player in the contemporary Scottish game to have any claims on being a world-class footballer. He seems to be without a weakness. He is quite brilliant in the air; an historic example of that was in Scotland's important World Cup qualifying match in Cyprus in 1989. Gough headed a superb goal from a corner kick in the very last minute, to give Scotland a desperate victory which, of course, incensed the Cypriot crowd. Richard is a sound tackler, with exceptionally sharp timing and excellent distribution. He is fast in recovery and in breaking forward into attack, very courageous and frighteningly strong in spite of his slender physique – 6 feet and 12 stone. In fact, Richard Gough looks as lean and dry and hard and brave as a Boer sharpshooter. With Rangers he formed a formidable central defensive partnership with Terry Butcher, whereas Scotland used him as a right-back. He could have elected to play for Sweden, South Africa or Scotland, but now has unlimited potential as a future Rangers and Scotland captain.

Games:	118
Goals:	10
League Championship:	1988–89, 1989–90
League Cup:	1987–88, 88–89
Honours:	50 Scotland caps
	(17 with Rangers)
Born:	Stockholm, 5 April 1962
Dundee United	
League Championship:	1982–83

RAY WILKINS
1987–89

A thoroughbred even as a teenager with Chelsea, Ray came to Ibrox with eighty–four England caps behind him and a career at the highest level of the game embracing Manchester United, AC Milan and Paris St Germain. Rangers paid the French club £250,000 for him, and it proved to be an excellent investment. As a footballer Wilkins was intelligent, dedicated, technically highly skilled and above all cool in temperament, perhaps his single outstanding characteristic. He played the role of anchorman in midfield, making himself a focal point which gathered balls from defence and moved them on to the advance players. Wilkins was a superb passer of the ball, particularly with the long pass from a rather deep position. He was inclined to play just in front of the defensive line and was criticised for not being more direct. He was rather conservative; indeed, Ron Atkinson, manager of Manchester United, dubbed him 'The Crab' because of his liking for the square pass.

If not a ball-winner as such, Ray was a good, firm tackler and an immensely creative player who would above all always seek to find the simple pass, the free receiver. He may well have vied with Graeme Souness as the finest midfield player Rangers have had since Baxter. Many people thought that highly of him, and when for family reasons he left Rangers in December 1989 to return to London with Queen's Park Rangers, he was given a farewell unsurpassed in Ibrox history. The entire ground, as they say, 'rose' to give Ray Wilkins a standing ovation.

Games:	96
Goals:	3
League Championship:	1988–89, 89–90
League Cup:	1988–89
Honours:	84 England caps
	(none with Rangers)
Born:	Hillingdon, 14 September 1956
Manchester United	
FA Cup:	1982–83

JOHN McGREGOR
1987–89

Signed in the summer of 1987, John had been given, rather surprisingly, a free transfer by Liverpool. He was first seen with Queen's Park in the early eighties, when many clubs, Rangers and Celtic included, showed interest in him. He decided on Liverpool, where he served a long apprenticeship. A serious leg injury while on loan to St Mirren, which recurred later while he was at Ibrox following a hard tackle by Stuart McKimmie at Aberdeen, cut short John's playing career. He was forced to retire, and joined the Rangers coaching staff.

Games: 33
Goals: 0
League Cup: 1987–88
Born: Airdrie, 5 January 1963

IAN McCALL
1987–90

A left-side midfield player, Ian joined from Dunfermline Athletic in September 1987 for £200,000, having previously been with Motherwell and Queen's Park. He was occasionally used in attack, but was never a regular first-team man. He fell foul of the management by failing to appear for a training session in December 1989. In January 1990 he was transferred to Bradford City for £200,000 – Rangers got their money back on this one.

Games: 24
Goals: 2
Born: Dumfries, 30 September 1964

GARY McSWEGAN
1987–

A young centre-forward who joined from school and came through Rangers Amateurs BC and the Ibrox system, Gary was developing and scoring goals in the youth and reserve teams when, in August 1989, his career received a dreadful blow. In a reserve game with Celtic, his leg was badly broken by a dreadful tackle from the Celtic goalkeeper Ian Andrews, who was ordered off.

Games: 2
Goals: 0
Born: Glasgow, 24 September 1970

MARK WALTERS
1987–

The first coloured player to play for Rangers in fifty years, Mark Walters came from Aston Villa for £500,000 in January 1988 and brought a mercurial talent with him. His ball skills were such that he could turn defenders inside out, and he was something of a master of the 'Ali Shuffle', fluttering his right foot over the ball. He boasted a tremendous shot, and the skill to chip or float the ball around or over goalkeepers. He was also menacing with free kicks from the fringes of the penalty area. Mark was, however, inconsistent, sometimes indolent, and tended to vanish if the going got rough, especially in away matches. He was a controversial figure, to a large extent because of his colour, but also because it was not unknown for him to retaliate. He was ordered off twice in his early Rangers years, both times against Hearts at Tynecastle. Graeme Souness tended to use him wide and somewhat withdrawn on either wing, although he had plenty of pace to go through the centre.

Games: 102
Goals: 36
League Championship: 1988–89, 89–90
League Cup: 1988–89
Born: Birmingham, 2 June 1964

MARK FALCO
1987–88

JOHN BROWN
1987–

Mark was a striker, a big fellow bought from Watford for £270,000 in the summer of 1987 and a player who certainly did not let Rangers down. He was strong and forceful, very good in the air, more mobile and more polished than, say, Colin West. An illustration of his coolness and quickness came from the first goal against Dynamo Kiev at Ibrox in 1987 in the European Champions Cup. A dreadful goalkeeping mistake made it possible, but Falco accepted the gift smartly and made quite sure of the conversion. He moved to Queen's Park Rangers after only a few months at Ibrox – one suspects reluctantly. It was a strange transfer, particularly since Robert Fleck moved to Norwich a month later, leaving Rangers with only one recognised striker eligible for European competition (the quarter-finals in fact). This may well have cost Rangers the tie, against Steau Bucharest, since Alistair McCoist had a cartilage operation only a matter of days beforehand.

Games:	19
Goals:	10
Born:	London, 22 October 1960
Tottenham Hotspur	
UEFA Cup:	1983–84

A capable, all-round utility player, John came from Dundee in January 1988 for £350,000. A strong tackler and reasonable user of the ball, he was a forceful, never-say-die redhead. He played full-back, central defence or even on the left of midfield, and had a rocketing shot which could bring goals from better than twenty–five yards when backing up his forwards. He was a goal-scorer against Rangers in his time, with the only and winning goal in a Scottish Cup tie at Ibrox in 1984, and a hat-trick in a League match in November 1985. These must have hurt – John is a lifelong 'Blue-nose'.

Games:	84
Goals:	7
League Championship:	1988–89, 89–90
League Cup:	1988–89
Born:	Stirling, 26 January 1962

JAN BARTRAM
1987–88

Jan had a short, controversial life with Rangers. A Danish international left-back, or left-side midfield player, he came from Silkeborg for £180,000, a fast and skilful player. Whilst on international duty with Denmark, he was reported to have been highly critical of Graeme Souness and his methods, and of Rangers. Later, of course, he denied these articles and their allegations, but his days were numbered and a few months later he was back in Denmark – he went to Bronby for £315,000.

Games:	14
Goals:	3
Honours:	2 Denmark caps (while with Rangers)
Born:	Denmark

GARY STEVENS
1988–

England's international right-back was another of Graeme Souness's seven-figure buys in July of 1988, when he paid Everton a round £1 million for the player. Gary enjoys the one asset full-backs must have above all others – speed – and it enables him to forage ahead on overlapping attacks yet remain confident in recovery. He took some time to settle to the Scottish game, and made few friends when he was clearly responsible for Celtic's winning goal in the 1989 Scottish Cup Final. His faulty pass back allowed Joe Miller to steal possession and take the solitary goal. With the advent of Trevor Steven, his former Everton club-mate, Gary looked much more settled in his work. In eight years at Everton he had won English League and Cup honours and a European Cup Winners' Cup Final against Rapid Vienna in Rotterdam.

Games:	96
Goals:	3
League Championship:	1988–89, 89–90
League Cup:	1988–89
Honours:	41 England caps (15 with Rangers)
Born:	Barrow-in-Furness, 27 March 1963
Everton	
FA Cup:	1983–84
Football League Championship:	1984–85, 86–87
European Cup Winners' Cup:	1984–85

TREVOR FRANCIS
1987–88

Trevor Francis joined Rangers late in his career from Atalanta in Italy, for £75,000. He had played in Italy with Graeme Souness, at Sampdoria of Genoa. Francis was an exceptional player, a vastly experienced England international footballer who played in a variety of forward positions. In his best years he had been a striker of killing pace and finish – witness the fact that he was the first £1 million footballer in Britain. From his native Plymouth he went to Birmingham City as a teenager, and Brian Clough paid that huge amount of money to take him to Nottingham Forest. At Ibrox he was used by Graeme Souness sparingly, always wide on the right, and judiciously, seldom being asked to play the full ninety minutes. His stunning first touch, his general ball control and close dribbling, and his accuracy with the ball delighted Rangers fans. His experience was invaluable to the club, but he left after his one-season contract to join Queen's Park Rangers where he became player–manager before moving on to Sheffield Wednesday.

Games:	25
Goals:	0
League Cup:	1987–88
Honours:	52 England caps
	(none with Rangers)
Born:	Plymouth, 19 April 1954
Nottingham Forest	
European Champions Cup:	1978–79
European Super Cup:	1979–80

IAN FERGUSON
1987–

Ian Ferguson, a powerful, hard-running midfield or forward player, was first noted at Clyde and was snapped up by St Mirren for £60,000 in 1986–87. He was noted even more when he scored a spectacular and, as it happened, winning goal for St Mirren against the more strongly fancied Dundee United in the 1987 Scottish Cup Final. This may have given Ferguson delusions of grandeur. In the following season, when it became known that Rangers wanted him, Ferguson reached a point when he could no longer play for St Mirren because, he said, of all the media pressure and speculation concerning his future. He also made it clear to St Mirren that he wanted to play for Rangers, despite the four-year contract he had with the Paisley club. He was bought by Rangers in February 1988 for £700,000. Many critics saw him as potentially one of the great players of the Scottish game. Others felt that a certain bitter element in his character might prevent that. He was very successful in 1988–89, scoring in the League Cup Final against Aberdeen, but his form slumped in 1989–90 as a result of injury and illness.

Games:	82
Goals:	16
League Championship:	1988–89, 89–90
League Cup:	1988–89
Honours:	3 Scotland caps
Born:	Glasgow, 15 March 1967
St Mirren	
Scottish Cup:	1986–87

KEVIN DRINKELL
1988–89

Much missed by Rangers fans after he had left, Kevin Drinkell spent only fifteen months at Ibrox, from the summer of 1988 to October 1989. He was signed from Norwich City for £500,000, having previously been with his home-town team, Grimsby. He was sold to Coventry City for £800,000, this representing good business for Rangers if nothing else, and indeed his transfer may simply have been a question of profit and liquidity. A big striker, strong in the air, mobile and very active, he was a goal-scorer who struck up a worthwhile finishing partnership with Alistair McCoist. In one sense he may have been a sacrifice, with the coming of Maurice Johnston.

Games:	54
Goals:	19
League Championship:	1988–89
League Cup:	1988–89
Born:	Grimsby, 18 June 1960

TOM COWAN
1988–

A left-back, Tom is a young man of outstanding potential. His rise was meteoric – he played only one season with Clyde before Rangers bought him for a hefty £100,000, and Tom Cowan is clearly seen as a star of the future.

Games:	8
Goals:	0
Born:	Bellshill, 28 August 1969

NEALE COOPER
1988–

As a young player, Neale Cooper, with Scottish international selections at youth and Under-21 levels, was reckoned to be a prospect as outstanding as Celtic's Paul McStay. Indeed, he was described by Franz Beckenbauer as the greatest prospect he had seen anywhere in the world at that age. His best position was clearly in central defence, but in his spell at Aberdeen in the early eighties, manager Alex Ferguson, with Willie Miller and Alec McLeish established in the central positions, sought to make Cooper a ball-winning midfield player. He was a ball-winner with a vengeance, with a reputation as one of the fiercest tacklers in football. He had much success at Pittodrie – four Scottish Cup, two League Championship, one League Cup and one European Cup Winners' Cup medals. Rangers signed him in October 1988 from Aston Villa for £250,000, no doubt as cover for all defensive positions. Injury compromised much of his contribution through much of 1989.

Games:	20
Goals:	1
League Cup:	1988–89
Born:	Darjeeling, India, 24 November 1963

Aberdeen	
Scottish Cup:	1981–82, 82–83, 83–84, 85–86
League Championship:	1983–84, 84–85
League Cup:	1985–86
European Cup Winners' Cup:	1982–83
European Super Cup:	1983–84

MEL STERLAND
1988–89

Mel arrived in March 1989 from Sheffield Wednesday, where he had been captain and where he had received a testimonial. A right full-back or midfield player, he cost Rangers £800,000. He was a lusty, yeoman type who was never played in his best position, that of full-back. He went to Leeds United in the summer of 1989, but not before leaving the Ibrox crowd with good memories in the shape of two goals in what was virtually the Championship-winning game, against Hearts at Ibrox in April.

Games:	13
Goals:	3
Honours:	1 England cap (not with Rangers)
Born:	Sheffield, 1 October 1961

ANDY GRAY
1988–89

Andrew Mullen Gray signed for Rangers in September 1988 for £25,000, surely bringing to an end a transfer trail that had involved him with half a dozen clubs and purchases worth a collective £2 million. He turned professional with Dundee United in May 1973, from schoolboy football. In September 1975 Aston Villa paid £110,000 for him, then in 1979 collected a then British record of a still-staggering £1.46 million from Wolverhampton Wanderers. Andy next moved to Everton, then Aston Villa again, and Rangers in fact signed him from West Bromwich Albion. With Everton he won English League, FA Cup and European Cup Winners' Cup honours. He played for Scotland at schoolboy, youth and Under-23 levels, and won twenty full caps.

He was a big centre-forward, tall and very fast for his size and brave as could be, this quality taking him into the tightest of situations and bringing the inevitable series of injuries. He was particularly good and courageous in the air, and played the game with the enthusiasm of a McCoist. He was used by Rangers mainly as a substitute, but as a Rangers fan himself, rejoiced in his time at Ibrox.

Games:	16
Goals:	5
Honours:	20 Scotland caps (none with Rangers)
Born:	Glasgow, 30 November 1955
Wolverhampton Wanderers	
Football League Cup:	1979–80
Everton	
Football League Championship:	1984–85
FA Cup:	1983–84
European Cup Winners' Cup:	1984–85

SANDY ROBERTSON
1987–

Son of the former Ayr United, Hearts and Dundee United player Malcolm Robertson, Sandy came on schoolboy forms, and as a midfield or forward player of good vision and good passing skills, with luck he should have a good career in the game.

Games:	3
Goals:	0
Born:	Edinburgh, 26 April 1971

TREVOR STEVEN
1989–

The subject of a transfer tribunal ruling (Everton valued him at £4.5 million), Trevor came to Rangers in the summer of 1989 from the Liverpool club for £1.7 million. Formerly with Burnley, he had won English Championship, Cup and European Cup Winners' Cup prizes with Everton and become an established England international player as a cultured right-winger or right midfield player. His partnership with Gary Stevens for Everton and England was resumed successfully for Rangers. Trevor took over the midfield role of Ray Wilkins and formed a telling combination with Nigel Spackman, Steven's calculated distribution marrying with Spackman's strength and exuberance.

Games:	43
Goals:	5
League Championship:	1989–90
Honours:	29 England caps (4 with Rangers)
Born:	Berwick, 21 October 1963
Burnley	
Football League	
Third Division Championship:	1981–82
Everton	
European Cup Winners' Cup:	1984–85
FA Cup:	1983–84
Football League Championship:	1984–85, 86–87

KEVIN MACDONALD
1988–89

Kevin came on a month's loan from Liverpool in the 1988–89 season. He was tall, slim, workmanlike, a midfield player who had previously been with Elgin City and Leicester City.

Games:	3
Goals:	0
Born:	Dufftown, 7 September 1959
Liverpool	
FA Cup:	1985–86

MAURICE JOHNSTON
1989–

Maurice Johnston, centre-forward, joined Rangers on 10 July 1989 for £1.5 million from the Nantes club in France. An established Scottish international player, 'Mo' had previously played for Partick Thistle, Watford and Celtic. His signing may be considered the most sensational in Scottish football history, since he was widely, if mistakenly, assumed to be the first Roman Catholic player to play for Rangers. He was, in all probability, the first Catholic to be a first-team player since the Second World War. A possible exception to that would be Don Kitchenbrand, the big South African of the fifties, who confessed, long after his career at Ibrox was over, to being a Catholic.

As a player Johnston was a proven goal-scorer at all his clubs, his pace and sharp reflexes taking him into the striking places. Surprisingly good and imaginative in the air for his height (5' 9"), he was a tireless worker, a chaser of lost causes, unselfish in his distribution and totally fearless. Johnston took the knocks, and since he played in ankle socks, spurning any shin protection, there were more of these than need be. His physical movement was so intense, so concentrated that it sometimes appeared feverish, even desperate, and there was precious little relaxation in his game.

Under all the circumstances, signing for Rangers showed great courage and strength of character on the part of Maurice Johnston. Many doubted that anyone could cope with the pressures, in a city like Glasgow, or that the Rangers fans would allow him to cope, but from the beginning he was accepted by almost all the Rangers players and almost all the fans. Some Rangers supporters, however, contemplating what was something of a historic event, still have strong reservations about Johnston's place at Ibrox.

Games:	45
Goals:	17
League Championship:	1989–90
Honours:	36 Scotland caps
	(8 with Rangers)
Born:	Glasgow, 13 April 1963
Celtic	
League Championship:	1985–86
Scottish Cup:	1984–85

DAVIE DODDS
1989–

Bought no doubt as cover for Alistair McCoist and Maurice Johnston, David Dodds brought with him a wealth of experience when he joined Rangers from Aberdeen in September 1989 for £100,000. Capped as a schoolboy and later at youth and Under-21 levels, he began his professional career with Dundee United in 1975 where he won full Scotland caps. In the summer of 1986 he moved to Xamax Neuchatel in Switzerland for £180,000, a move which was unsuccessful and saw him back with Aberdeen that September for a fee of £215,000. Only Alistair McCoist and Frank McGarvey have scored more Premier Division goals than Dodds. While with Dundee United he made a habit of scoring against Rangers – nine goals in League games alone. A tall, rather awkward mover, nevertheless he is very mobile for his size, very clever in the air, and very adept at holding a forward line together and in laying off the ball.

Games:	15
Goals:	4
Honours:	2 Scotland caps
	(none with Rangers)
Born:	Dundee, 23 September 1958

Dundee United	
League Cup:	1980–81
League Championship:	1982–83

CHRIS VINNICOMBE
1989–

In spite of the attentions of many English clubs, Liverpool included, Chris signed for Rangers in a £100,000 transfer which will require the Ibrox club to pay Exeter City additional amounts depending on the young man's progress. Vinnicombe is a left-side player of slim build, rather like Tom Cowan, and he has high potential as an attacking player.

Games:	8
Goals:	0
Born:	Exeter, 20 October 1970

NIGEL SPACKMAN
1989–

Nigel joined from Queen's Park Rangers in December 1989. A solid, hard-working midfield player, he made himself something of an instant folk-hero by scoring the only goal against Celtic at Parkhead on 2 January 1990 for the first Rangers win there in the New Year match for more than twenty years. A ball-winner, and difficult to knock off the ball once he has possession, Nigel has formed an impressive midfield partnership with Trevor Steven.

Games:	23
Goals:	1
League Championship:	1989–90
Born:	Romney, 2 December 1960

Liverpool	
Football League Championship:	1987–88

BEN Z. GINSBURG
1989–

'Bonnie' Ginsburg, Israeli international goalkeeper, joined Rangers in August 1989 from Maccabi Tel Aviv. Courageous and quick off his line when needs be, he made a rather uncertain start in Scottish football, losing two rather soft goals to Hibs at Easter Road in an early match, but since then he has proved more than an adequate reserve to Chris Woods. Many Rangers fans believe he should be first-choice goalkeeper.

Games:	8
Shutouts:	4
Honours:	2 Israel caps
	(while with Rangers)
Born:	Tel Aviv, 12 December 1964

THE MANAGERS

William Struth

William Struth, manager of Rangers from 1920 to 1954, was born in Edinburgh. He was a stonemason by trade, which no doubt helped to make him physically strong. As a young man he was a 'pedestrian', a professional runner who did the rounds of the tracks up and down the country, running for money as and where it was available. He became trainer of Clyde FC in 1908, then of Rangers in 1914.

On the death of the club's secretary–manager William Wilton – by drowning at Gourock in 1920 – Struth became secretary–manager. In the thirty-four years that followed, until he retired at the end of season 1953–54 and became vice-chairman of the club, Rangers won eighteen League Championships, ten Scottish Cup Finals and two League Cup Finals; the club won the Glasgow Cup eighteen times, the Glasgow Charity Cup twenty times. In season 1929–30 Rangers won every competition entered – Scottish Cup, League Championship, Reserve Cup, Reserve Championship, Glasgow and Glasgow Charity Cups.

Struth's record speaks for itself. If it is rivalled in any way, that would surely be by the Celtic successes of Jock Stein – nine Championships, seven Scottish Cups and six League Cups from 1965–75. And for longevity in the manager's chair, Struth can be spoken of only alongside his contemporaries, Willie Maley of Celtic and John Hunter of Motherwell.

He was a disciplinarian and a dandy – both elements of his character which were impressed upon the club. Struth never had much to say about the playing of the game, about tactics, about how to handle peculiarities in the opposition from week to week. That was left to his senior players and captains, players such as Tommy Muirhead, David Meiklejohn and George Young, who would guide the younger men. But behaviour and appearances were paramount. Struth had a network of informer friends of the club all over the country, and few Rangers players misbehaved without being discovered. Few avoided the consequences, which were an invitation to go 'up the stair' to Struth's office and a session in which the offender was (metaphorically) pinned to the wall. And the extremists who didn't listen closely enough would one way or another presently leave the club.

Struth kept half a dozen or more suits – all of them double-breasted – in his office at Ibrox, and might change two or three times a day. And he saw to it that Rangers players were all properly turned out, from the bowler hat and spats of the twenties to the post-1945 club blazer and slacks.

William Struth became director–manager of the club in 1947, retired as manager in the summer of 1954, and died on 21 September 1956 at the age of eighty-one. He was buried in Craigton Cemetery in Glasgow, a stone's throw from the club and the stadium which had been his life's work.

Scot Symon

By any reasonable standards, Scot Symon was an outstanding success as a football club manager. When he retired from playing at the end of season 1946–47, he became manager of East Fife. In his first season they were promoted to the First Division, or Division A as it was then called. In 1949–50 this little provincial club won the League Cup. Also in 1949–50 they reached the final of the Scottish Cup and faced Rangers, losing 3–0 to an outstanding

display by the winners, who scored in seconds. Symon moved to Preston North End in March 1953, saw that team into an FA Cup Final at Wembley, where they lost to West Bromwich Albion, then was invited back to Ibrox in June 1954 when Bill Struth vacated the managerial chair.

At Ibrox his success continued. The Championship was won in 1956, '57, '59 '61, '63, '64; the Scottish Cup was won in 1960, '62, '63, '64, '66 and the League Cup in 1961, '62, '64 and '65. The early sixties saw an exceptional Rangers team including Baxter and McMillan, Greig and McKinnon. Rangers were twice finalists in the European Cup Winners' Cup, in 1961 and 1967.

Scot Symon was the last of the lounge-suit managers, the waistcoat managers. He was never a track-suit man, never a man for working much on tactics. He let playing systems emerge from the talents of his players rather than imposing tactical systems on them. And he signed some extremely good players, excellent buys for the club. Scot was a shy man, by no means a media performer, essentially a man of his time, a man of the thirties. And, of course, Rangers do not operate simply to 'reasonable standards'. Scot Symon left Rangers on 1 November 1967, when they were top of the League, having won six and drawn two of the eight matches played. On that very day Celtic, European Cup holders, were playing in South America for the World Club Championship with the team that was to dominate the rest of the decade.

Perhaps it was the correct decision by the club to change managers. Perhaps they needed a more contemporary figure – Symon was an old-school gentleman, and he was fifty-eight. More and more, football club management was being seen as a young man's game. But the manner of his going brought no credit to the board of directors. Clearly John Lawrence, the chairman, should have spoken to Symon personally, informally, perhaps seeking his counsel in the first place on the appointment of a team manager, suggesting that he, Symon, should become general manager with a seat on the board. After all, the man had been a tremendous servant to the club, both on and off the field. Instead, Lawrence sent a business associate who had no involvement with football nor with the club to do it for him. Symon, a proud man, not surprisingly 'took the huff' in the time-honoured phrase and would have none of it. He quit. He was briefly a director of Dumbarton, then manager of Partick Thistle.

David White

David White played wing-half for Clyde and, a Glasgow boy, spent his entire career with the Shawfield club. He became player–coach, then in 1966 manager of Clyde, and in 1967, when both Rangers and Celtic were in the finals of European competitions, Davie travelled with both clubs on observer, 'educational' trips. Perhaps he impressed the Rangers people. On their return from their Nuremburg final he was appointed assistant manager by Scot Symon. Five months later, with the departure of Symon, Davie White was manager of Rangers.

He had virtually no success in his two years at Ibrox – one Glasgow Cup victory amounted to nothing in the eyes of the faithful. He was perhaps desperately unlucky to have to contend with the astonishing Celtic team of Jock Stein, and the disappearance from the team of Baxter and McMillan. In season 1967–68, for example, Rangers were unbeaten going into their thirty-fourth and final League game against Aberdeen at Ibrox. They lost a League match for the only time that season, finished with 61 points, yet had to cede the Championship to Celtic, by two points.

In European football, White's Rangers in successive seasons reached the quarter-finals and the semi-finals of the Inter Cities Fairs Cup, but lost to Leeds United and Newcastle United respectively. White had the team playing quite well, even stylishly at times, but when it came to the clinching of a championship or a cup, bad luck always seemed to be on hand. In the 1969 Scottish Cup Final, scarcely credible defensive mistakes by experienced players invited Celtic to run all over them, which Celtic did 4–0. It was Rangers' heaviest Cup Final defeat. A goalkeeping fumble by Gerry Neef cost them a 1–0 defeat by Celtic at Parkhead and dismissal from the League Cup the following season.

White was perhaps not a disciplinarian. The players' dress was often sloppy, training sessions were missed and feeble excuses accepted. The end came for Davie White with the double defeat by Gornik Zabrze in November 1969, in the European Cup Winners' Cup. In the first match in Poland it was immediately obvious that the young manager had underestimated Gornik, saying in advance that Rangers would go all out in attack. They did – they were two goals down in twelve minutes and lost 3–1. In the second match at Ibrox, two goals in twelve minutes were again lost – this time the closing twelve minutes – and it was Gornik again, 3–1 again. That evening the Rangers board met, and next day David White was a former Rangers manager. He later managed Dundee to a League Cup victory. It may well be that Davie lacked the years, the maturity, the tactical and international experience for a job which is unlike any other in football.

Willie Waddell

Willie Waddell finished playing in the summer of 1956 and a year later was manager of Kilmarnock. In eight years there he brought surprising success to the provincial club – a Championship victory of all things, in 1964–65; a Scottish Cup Final (0–2 v Rangers in 1960) and two League Cup Finals (0–2 v Rangers in 1960–61 and 0–1 v Hearts in 1962–63). He became manager of Rangers on 3 December 1969. Thirteen months later, he faced what he may have come to believe was the greatest challenge of his public life.

On 2 January 1971, Rangers drew 1–1 with Celtic at Ibrox before a crowd of 80,000 people. In a match without any unruly incident, on the field or on the terraces, Jimmy Johnstone had scored for Celtic in the very last minute, only to see Colin Stein equalise with just fifteen seconds left to play. Rangers fans, spilling down Stairway 13 from the huge terraces, met disaster. One fan, riding on another's shoulders, toppled forward near the top of the exit staircase. The domino effect sent the huge crowd sprawling down the stairway. The result was that sixty-six people were crushed to death and 145 injured in one of football's worst disasters.

With a board of directors that seemed so stunned as to be ineffectual, Waddell took command. Two days later Rangers contributed £50,000 to the Lord Provost's Appeal Fund for the relatives. Waddell saw to it that the club was represented at each of the sixty-six funerals. The players, and many former players, were summoned and ordered to take part. But most of all, Waddell was haunted by the thought that the same thing might easily happen again.

It was time to make changes to an Ibrox which was huge, aged and in fact obsolete. He researched the modern grounds in Germany and elsewhere throughout Europe and

beyond, and within the decade Waddell had transformed Ibrox into probably the most attractive and sophisticated football stadium in Britain. It is a magnificent monument to the man. True, he was aided by Rangers Pools, which provided some of the £10 million funding (it invariably produces a seven-figure gift to the club each year). But Willie Waddell had done it – crabbit or not, he had done it. He was an achiever. He got things done – on the field, at Kilmarnock, in journalism, as a Rangers player, as a Rangers executive. And he was a visionary. He brought in Jock Wallace as coach, and in June of 1972 made him team manager. It was the beginning of better days for the Light Blues.

Jock Wallace

Jock Wallace, from Wallyford in Midlothian, was a hard man, often called 'Rock' Wallace if seldom to his face, and he had a remarkable, far-travelled career in the old game. Not many men could envisage being manager of Rangers. Wallace was, twice. Not many managers in Scotland can envisage winning the treble of League, Scottish Cup and League Cup. Wallace did it, twice.

A goalkeeper, he played first for Airdrie and was transferred to West Bromwich Albion for £8000 in 1959. From there he moved to Bedford, Hereford and Berwick. Indeed, on that most fateful of all days in Rangers' history, 28 January 1967, Jock Wallace was in the Berwick goal in their first-round Scottish Cup tie, when the Rangers of Berwick beat the Rangers of Glasgow 1–0. There were many consequences of that result. As player–manager of the border club, he made them promotion chasers within a couple of years. In 1968 he went to Hearts as assistant to manager John Harvey, and in June 1970 Willie Waddell, a good judge of abrasive characters, took him to Ibrox as coach. In June 1972 he was appointed team manager. He resigned in May 1978 and joined Leicester City. In 1982 he was back in Scotland to manage and help consolidate the promoted Motherwell. He succeeded John Greig at Ibrox in November 1983 and was sacked in April 1986 by David Holmes, chief executive, no doubt to make way for Graeme Souness. Jock then went to the Seville club in Spain, later returning to manage Colchester United. These are the bare bones of his career.

Jock Wallace was a hard man, a hard taskmaster, a motivator supreme who, in his time in National Service with the King's Own Scottish Borderers, had served in Northern Ireland, and had fought Communist insurgents in the jungles of Malaysia. His training methods were sometimes controversial – at one time he had Rangers players running up and down the huge sand dunes at Gullane. Yet this brought them bursting fitness and was probably a foundation for the long careers which players such as Sandy Jardine, Alex Macdonald, Tommy McLean, Alex Miller, John Greig, Colin Jackson and others enjoyed. And he brought on young players in the seventies such as Derek Johnstone, Bobby Russell and Alistair Dawson, all of whom had long careers. A further testament to the Wallace teaching methods was the number of these players who went into management.

He was tactically shrewd. As coach in 1970–71, his League Cup win over Celtic, even if a narrow 1–0, dented if it did not end the dominance of Jock Stein's team. As manager he won the Centenary Scottish Cup in 1973, against Celtic again, this time by 3–2. There was the European Cup Winners' Cup success in 1972, then came the winning of the Championship in 1974–75, for the first time in eleven years.

With this impetus came the winning of the treble of League, Scottish Cup and League Cup, in 1975–76 and again in 1977–78. It was the first time in Scottish football history that any manager had done this. But only a matter of days after completing the second treble, with a 2–1 Scottish Cup Final win over Aberdeen on 23 May 1978, Jock Wallace shocked Scottish football by resigning. John Greig was named manager the next day.

The reasons for Wallace's departure from Ibrox have never been publicly explained, but a clash of personality with Willie Waddell, even amid all that success, is usually accepted as the cause. Waddell had brought Wallace to Ibrox as coach. He had made him team manager on 7 June 1972 when he, Waddell, became general manager. The general opinion seems to be that Waddell would not release money that Wallace had decided was necessary to reinforce the team. Waddell, it should be said, was very much involved in the design, construction and funding of the new stadium at this time.

Wallace took off for Leicester City and took them to the Championship of the Second Division of the Football League, and to a place in the FA Cup semi-finals. There was no doubt that this man knew the business of running a football team. He was back north in the summer of 1982 with Motherwell, and eighteen months later, following the resignation of John Greig, returned to Ibrox. Jock brought new life to what was an ailing team, with a long, unbeaten run. Rangers won the League Cup in March of 1984, beating Celtic in the final 3–2, and the 1984–85 final against Dundee United, 1–0. But the team never did challenge for the Championship. Aberdeen and Dundee United had become powers in the land. Indeed, season 1985–86 could be said to have been the worst in Rangers' League Championship history. It was the only season in its existence in which the club failed to average at least one point per match.

When the John Lawrence organisation bought out enough of the Rangers shareholdings to give them control of the club, changes may have been inevitable and extra pressure would have fallen on Wallace. As it was, an abysmal 2–0 defeat by Tottenham Hotspur in April 1986 saw Wallace sacked by David Holmes, a John Lawrence appointee and chief executive of the Rangers club. Jock Wallace, undaunted, took himself off to Seville to manage the Spanish club, then returned first to manage Colchester United, then to become a director of the Essex club.

John Greig

There is an old football saw which insists that promoting a player directly from the dressing room to the manager's chair, as it were, never quite works. More often than not, that is true, and the experience of Kenny Dalglish and the Liverpool club may simply be the exception which proves the rule. Alas, it was certainly true in the case of John Greig, one of the greatest of all Rangers players.

John was appointed manager of Rangers on 24 May 1978, the day after Jock Wallace left Ibrox, first time round. He inherited the 'Treble Team' of 1977–78 – Wallace's second treble as a manager, Greig's unprecedented third as a player. John had played a total of forty-one matches that season.

With a squad of experienced and successful players to hand, with his knowledge of the club, its ways and its

history, there was no reason to suppose that John Greig the manager might not maintain this success. The team won the League Cup and the Scottish Cup, the final of which required three games against Hibernian, and in the European Champions Cup disposed of Juventus and PSV Eindhoven before going down to Cologne in the quarter-final. The Championship was lost to Celtic at Parkhead in a decisive game by 4–2. Five minutes from the end, Colin Jackson inadvertently headed into his own goal, and in the very last minute Murdo MacLeod whacked in the fourth. Celtic took the title by three points. In hindsight, it was an ominous failure by Greig's team.

His second season, 1979–80, was something of a near-disaster. Rangers finished fifth in the Championship. All season long they failed to beat Celtic in any competitive game. They went out of the League Cup at the third round, beaten home and away by Aberdeen. Greig indulged in a flurry of buying and selling. Ian Redford came from Dundee for £210,000, Gregor Stevens from Leicester City for £150,000; Derek Parlane went to Leeds United for £160,000. The team did get to the Scottish Cup Final, the one hope of salvaging something from the season, and faced Celtic in another critical match. A good open game ran true to what was becoming the Greig form – seventeen minutes into extra time, George McCluskey diverted a Danny McGrain shot which McCloy had covered, and Celtic had won, 1–0. Gordon Smith's move to Brighton brought in £400,000; Colin MacAdam cost a 'tribunal' fee of £165,000 from Partick Thistle, Jim Bett £180,000 from the Lokeren club in Belgium.

The next season, 1980–81, saw Rangers make a bright opening of an unbeaten run over the first fifteen matches. Aberdeen again dumped them out of the League Cup, and in the Scottish Cup they overcame Dundee United 4–1 in a replayed final. But still the League was beyond them – they finished third.

At the end of season 1981–82, experienced players such as Sandy Jardine, Colin Jackson and Tommy McLean left the club. Rangers won the League Cup again, reached the Scottish Cup final for the seventh successive year, yet lost to Aberdeen after extra time, and yet again could do no better than third in the Championship. This continuing failure in the League was beginning to irk the many friends of Rangers – which was reflected in Ibrox attendances. In 1982–83 Greig paid Hibs a record £225,000 for Craig Paterson, but Rangers finished fourth in the Championship, no fewer than eighteen points behind the champions, Dundee United. John Greig resigned on 28 October 1983, saying 'I've finished with the game!' – exactly what many men would say in a moment of pique, a time of frustration. In early 1990 he did come back to the game, back to the club, as manager of public relations for Rangers, a rather less fearsome post than that of manager.

A certain amount of detachment is needed by football managers. When a man has spent some sixteen years as one of the boys in the dressing room downstairs, and is pitched upstairs at a day's notice, he must find it difficult to establish a code of discipline to apply to his friends. Failure to do that may have been the fate that befell John Greig.

Graeme Souness

As Rangers' very first player–manager, Graeme James Souness may yet make a greater contribution to Scottish football then he ever did on the field despite fifty-four caps and captaincy of his country. Since he took control of the management of the Rangers team in April 1986, he has revolutionised the Scottish game. By spending vast amounts, by Scottish standards, on buying players and importing high-quality English players, enticing them no doubt with huge salaries and the prospect of playing in European competitions from which English clubs have been banned, Souness reversed the trend of a century or more, when the norm was that Scottish players went to England to seek greater reward.

Thanks to an earlier manager, and managing director, of Rangers, Willie Waddell, Rangers already had a modern, magnificent stadium in the mid eighties. The Souness ambition was clearly to make the team match the stadium, and if it took a cosmopolitan recruiting policy to do that, so be it. His avowed aim was for Rangers to win a European competition. When the call came from David Holmes, then chairman of the club, in the late spring of 1986, Graeme Souness was ready. He had a mass of international experience and playing achievement behind him with Scotland, of national and European experience with Liverpool, and the direct personal experience of playing at the highest level of Italian football, perhaps the most sophisticated footballing atmosphere in the world.

But before settling into the new job came the World Championship finals in Mexico that summer. Souness, the captain, was left out of the team for the final critical group match against Uruguay, an error of judgement on the part of Alex Ferguson, the international team manager, to which he later confessed at a huge charity lunch in Glasgow, apologising publicly to Souness, who was present.

To complete a remarkable story in the remarkable fortunes of this Rangers club, Graeme Souness and a friend, David Murray, bought control of the club from the Lawrence organisation in 1989. Murray was a self-made millionaire with interests in metal stockholding and property, and one of a new wave of young Scottish entrepreneurs. He was thus into the wider management of the club and looked like a potential contender for Bill Struth's record of service as a manager. Although still registered as a player, he has become preoccupied more and more with management.

STATISTICS

		LEAGUE App Gl	SCOTTISH CUP App Gl	LEAGUE CUP App Gl	EUROPE App Gl	TOTAL App Gl
Alexander, T.	70–71	2–0	0–0	0–0	0–0	2–0
Anderson, S.	59–60	1–0	0–0	0–0	0–0	1–0
Armour, D.	74–79	3–0	0–0	1–0	0–0	4–0
Arnison, N.	55–57	0–0	0–0	2–2	0–0	2–2
Arnison, W.	46–47	7–1	1–0	2–3	0–0	10–4
Austin, A.	57–58	1–0	0–0	0–0	0–0	1–0
Baillie, D.	60–64	31–0	4–0	3–0	2–0	40–0
Baird, S.	55–61	121–39	16–2	26–6	16–5	179–52
Bartram, J.	87–88	11–3	3–0	0–0	0–0	14–3
Baxter, J.	60–65, 69–70	150–19	21–0	54–2	29–3	254–24
Beattie, S.	85–87	5–0	0–0	0–0	0–0	5–0
Beck, T.	64–65	11–2	2–0	1–0	0–0	14–2
Beckett, W.	50–51	1–0	0–0	0–0	0–0	1–0
Bell, D.	85–87	35–1	0–0	4–0	5–0	44–1
Bett, J.	80–83	104–21	18–2	24–6	6–1	152–30
Black, K.	81–84	23–1	3–0	7–1	0–0	33–2
Bonnyman, P.	72–73	0–0	0–0	1–0	0–0	1–0
Boyd, G.	75–76	1–0	0–0	0–0	0–0	1–0
Boyd, W.	51–52	2–0	0–0	0–0	0–0	2–0
Brand, R.	54–65	206–127	33–29	54–38	24–12	317–206
Brown, J.	87–	65–4	12–3	6–0	1–0	84–7
Brown, R.	46–56	211–0	33–0	52–0	0–0	296–0
Bruce, A.	81–86	2–0	0–0	0–0	0–0	2–0
Burns, H.	83–87	52–4	1–0	8–0	2–0	63–4
Butcher, T.	86–	122–8	11–0	18–0	16–2	167–10
Caldow, E.	53–66	265–17	39–4	68–1	35–3	407–25
Caskie, J.	46–49	26–3	4–0	9–2	0–0	39–5
Christie, J.	61–62	3–3	0–0	4–3	1–2	8–8
Clark, R.	80–82	1–0	0–0	0–0	0–0	1–0
Clark, S.	82–85	41–13	7–2	10–5	4–1	62–21
Cohen, A.	86–88	7–0	0–0	2–0	3–0	12–0
Conn, A.	68–74	91–23	13–3	31–11	11–2	146–39
Cooper, D.	77–89	376–44	49–7	77–18	38–1	540–70
Cooper, N.	88–	17–1	2–0	1–0	0–0	20–1
Cowan, T.	88–	7–0	0–0	0–0	1–0	8–0
Cox, S.	46–55	207–12	40–3	63–3	0–0	310–18
Cunning, R.	54–55	3–0	0–0	2–0	0–0	5–0
Dalziel, G.	78–84	33–9	8–1	6–1	0–0	47–11
Davies, B.	80–86	11–1	3–0	5–0	2–1	21–2
Davis, H.	56–64	168–8	23–0	42–3	28–2	261–13
Dawson, A.	75–87	218–7	36–0	39–1	23–1	316–9
Denny, J.	70–79	37–0	3–0	21–0	5–0	66–0
Dodds, D.	89–	14–4	1–0	0–0	0–0	15–4
Donaldson, G.	72–74	5–0	0–0	5–0	0–0	10–0
Drinkell, K.	88–89	36–11	8–5	6–2	4–1	54–19
Duncan, G.	57–60	12–5	2–0	1–0	0–0	15–5
Duncanson, J.	46–51	93–41	17–7	30–11	0–0	140–59
Dunlop, R.	50–53	3–0	0–0	0–0	0–0	3–0
Durrant, I.	84–	122–18	5–3	19–5	14–3	160–29
Elliott, A.	55–56	2–0	0–0	0–0	0–0	2–0
Falco, M.	87–88	14–5	0–0	3–3	2–2	19–10
Ferguson, A.	67–69	42–25	6–0	10–4	9–6	67–35
Ferguson, D.	82–90	111–7	8–0	11–1	15–1	145–9
Ferguson, E.	83–86	13–1	0–0	0–0	0–0	13–1
Ferguson, Iain	84–86	33–6	1–0	8–3	4–2	46–11
Ferguson, Ian	87–	61–9	7–2	8–4	6–1	82–16
Findlay, W.	47–54	70–37	11–7	33–21	0–0	114–65
Fleck, R.	83–88	85–29	3–0	8–2	8–3	104–34
Forrest, J.	62–67	106–83	10–6	37–50	11–6	164–145
Forsyth, A.	78–81	25–5	1–0	8–0	7–0	41–5
Forsyth, T.	72–82	218–2	36–2	50–2	20–0	324–6
Frame, J.	48–52	1–0	0–0	0–0	0–0	1–0
Francis, T.	87–88	18–0	1–0	2–0	4–0	25–0
Franks, A.	59–60	3–0	0–0	0–0	0–0	3–0
Fraser, C.	84–87	51–6	3–1	12–2	8–0	74–9
Fraser, S	83–85	9–0	1–0	0–0	0–0	10–0
Fyfe, G.	69–76	61–21	1–0	20–9	5–1	87–31
Gardiner, W.	51–55	25–16	3–2	3–1	0–0	31–19
Gillick, T.	46–50	104–49	16–5	20–8	0–0	140–62
Ginsberg, Ben Z.	89–	4–0	0–0	3–0	1–0	8–0
Gough, R.	87–	92–8	10–0	9–1	7–1	118–10
Gray, A.	88–89	14–5	1–0	1–0	0–0	16–5
Gray, D.	46–47	9–0	0–0	3–0	0–0	12–0
Grant, R.	59–60	1–0	0–0	0–0	0–0	1–0
Greig, J.	61–78	498–87	72–9	121–17	62–7	753–120
Grierson, D.	52–57	72–42	13–6	21–11	0–0	106–59
Hamilton, J.	73–78	59–5	11–2	5–1	1–0	76–8
Henderson, M.	74–78	33–10	5–3	5–1	3–0	46–14
Henderson, W.	60–72	276–36	44–5	60–11	46–10	426–62
Heron, B.	69–70	7–0	0–0	0–0	2–0	9–0
Hogg, W.	57–59	2–1	0–0	0–0	0–0	2–1
Houston, D.	73–74	10–0	0–0	4–0	3–0	17–0
Hubbard, J.	49–59	172–76	19–5	41–22	6–1	238–104
Hume, R.	59–62	17–3	3–0	0–0	3–0	23–3
Hunter, D.	73–75	3–0	1–0	0–0	0–0	4–0

STATISTICS

		LEAGUE App Gl	SCOTTISH CUP App Gl	LEAGUE CUP App Gl	EUROPE App Gl	TOTAL App Gl
Hunter, W.	62–66	1–0	0–0	0–0	0–0	1–0
Hynd, R.	63–69	31–4	4–1	6–0	7–0	48–5
Jackson, C.	63–82	341–23	54–8	75–8	36–1	506–40
Jardine, W.	65–82	450–42	64–8	107–24	50–2	671–76
Johansen, K.	65–70	158–4	21–2	32–2	27–1	238–9
Johnson, J.	47–52	32–11	2–2	2–1	0–0	36–14
Johnston, M.	89–	36–15	2–1	5–1	2–0	45–17
Johnston, W.	64–73, 80–82	245–91	43–10	65–17	40–8	393–126
Johnstone, D.	70–83, 84–86	372–131	57–30	84–39	31–9	547–209
Kennedy, A.	82–84	15–3	3–1	2–0	0–0	20–4
Kennedy, S.	73–80	99–0	10–0	19–0	3–0	131–0
King, R.	61–62	2–0	0–0	0–0	1–0	3–0
Kirkwood, D.	86–89	7–0	0–0	1–0	2–0	10–0
Kitchenbrand, D.	55–58	29–26	3–2	3–1	2–1	37–30
Liddell, C.	51–55	35–8	6–2	11–2	0–0	52–12
Lindsay, J.	46–52	17–0	1–0	4–0	0–0	22–0
Little, A.	47–51	6–0	0–0	0–0	0–0	6–0
Little J.	50–61	178–1	32–0	55–0	10–0	275–1
Logie, W.	56–57	16–0	0–0	0–0	3–0	19–0
Lyall, K.	81–84	8–0	1–0	2–0	0–0	11–0
Macdonald, A.	68–81	335–51	50–15	78–18	37–8	500–92
Macdonald, I.	69–73	11–2	1–0	2–0	0–0	14–2
Macdonald, J.	78–86	160–45	24–13	34–15	9–5	227–78
Macdonald, K.	88–89	3–0	0–0	0–0	0–0	3–0
Macfarlane, D.	84–89	7–0	1–0	1–0	0–0	9–0
McAdam, C.	80–85	65–15	12–8	19–9	3–0	99–32
McCall, I.	87–90	21–2	1–0	1–0	1–0	24–2
McCallum, A.	70–71	1–0	0–0	0–0	0–0	1–0
McClelland, J.	81–85	96–4	13–1	30–2	14–1	153–8
McCloy, P.	70–86	351–0	55–0	86–0	41–0	533–0
McCoist, A.	83–	225–133	21–10	38–31	23–7	307–181
McColl, I.	46–61	360–11	59–1	100–2	7–0	526–14
McCulloch, W.	49–55	49–9	14–5	5–1	0–0	68–15
McDougall, I.	73–77	31–3	2–0	3–0	1–0	37–3
McEwan, A.	58–59	1–0	0–0	0–0	0–0	1–0
McGregor, J.	87–89	25–0	0–0	4–0	4–0	33–0
McIntyre, John	49–50	2–0	0–0	0–0	0–0	2–0
McIntyre, James	81–82	1–0	0–0	0–0	0–0	1–0
McKean, R.	74–78	90–12	8–4	15–1	5–0	118–17
McKenzie, George	54–55	1–0	0–0	2–0	0–0	3–0
McKenzie, Gordon	54–55	9–0	0–0	0–0	0–0	9–0
McKinnon, D.	82–86	102–1	7–0	23–2	9–0	141–3
McKinnon, R.	60–72	301–2	44–0	83–0	45–1	473–3
McLean, G.	59–62	8–3	0–0	0–0	0–0	8–3
McLean, G.	62–67	68–49	14–8	28–23	6–2	116–82
McLean, T.	71–82	299–35	51–10	69–8	30–4	449–57
McMinn, K.	84–87	63–2	0–0	6–2	6–0	75–5
McMillan, H.	53–56	5–1	0–0	3–1	0–0	8–2
McMillan, I.	58–64	127–37	23–5	22–6	22–7	194–55
McNee, C.	46–47	10–3	0–0	0–0	0–0	10–3
McPhee, W.	68–70	1–0	0–0	2–0	0–0	3–0
McPherson, D.	81–87	163–15	15–3	28–2	16–6	222–26
McPherson, J.	47–48	1–1	0–0	0–0	0–0	1–1
McSwegan, G.	87–	2–0	0–0	0–0	0–0	2–0
Mackay, W.	75–85	24–1	2–0	7–2	3–1	36–4
Marshall, D.	46–53	14–7	0–0	6–2	0–0	20–9
Martin, N.	58–70	74–0	6–0	14–0	15–0	109–0
Mason, J.	72–74	16–2	1–0	2–0	0–0	19–2
Mathieson, W.	64–75	174–2	36–0	38–0	26–1	274–3
Matthew, A.	58–60	28–7	3–2	4–1	2–2	37–12
Melrose, H.	57–58	0–0	0–0	1–2	0–0	1–2
Menzies, R.	54–55	0–0	0–0	1–0	0–0	1–0
Millar, J.	54–67	197–92	35–30	54–27	31–11	317–160
Miller, A.	67–83	197–17	27–1	63–12	18–0	305–30
Miller, C.	85–87	2–0	1–0	0–0	0–0	3–0
Mitchell, D.	83–85	26–6	3–1	11–3	5–4	45–14
Moles, W.	57–58	3–0	0–0	2–0	0–0	5–0
Morris, E.	73–79	8–0	2–1	1–0	0–0	11–1
Morrison, R.	56–58	5–6	2–1	1–0	0–0	8–7
Munro, I.	76–77	5–0	0–0	6–1	0–0	11–1
Munro, S.	83–	165–3	12–0	20–0	16–0	213–3
Murray, M.	55–63	103–80	16–19	27–19	8–3	154–121
Neef, G.	68–73	33–0	3–0	6–0	6–0	48–0
Neillands, I.	51–52	6–0	1–1	0–0	0–0	7–1
Nicholl, J.	83–84, 86–89	74–0	7–0	14–0	11–0	106–0
Nisbet, S.	85–	45–1	2–0	2–1	7–0	56–2
Niven, G.	51–60	221–0	32–0	59–0	15–0	327–0
O'Hara, A.,	73–77	32–7	3–0	6–1	4–2	45–10
Orr, R.	58–59	1–0	0–0	0–0	0–0	1–0
Parlane, D.	70–80	201–80	25–8	51–21	19–2	296–111
Parlane, J.	46–48	5–3	2–0	0–0	0–0	7–3
Paterson, C.	82–87	83–4	8–0	26–5	13–3	130–12
Paterson, W.	58–62	67–0	12–0	19–0	18–0	116–0
Paton, W.	47–57	111–38	24–9	30–18	0–0	165–65
Paul, W.	66–67	1–0	0–0	0–0	0–0	1–0

STATISTICS

		LEAGUE App Gl	SCOTTISH CUP App Gl	LEAGUE CUP App Gl	EUROPE App Gl	TOTAL App Gl
Penman, A.	67–73	101–36	12–4	19–7	18–2	150–49
Penman, W.	60–61	3–0	0–0	0–0	0–0	3–0
Persson, O.	67–70	71–22	10–3	14–4	17–2	112–31
Phillips, J.	86–89	25–0	0–0	4–0	4–0	33–0
Prentice, J.	50–56	96–18	16–7	30–11	0–0	142–36
Provan, D.	58–70	170–9	20–1	50–1	22–0	262–11
Pryde, W.	53–55	11–0	2–0	0–0	0–0	13–0
Prytz, R.	82–85	78–12	11–1	19–5	10–2	118–20
Queen, J.	55–58	2–0	0–0	0–0	0–0	2–0
Rae, W.	46–57	130–6	16–0	33–1	0–0	179–7
Redford, I.	80–86	172–23	22–5	40–11	13–3	247–42
Reid, A.	66–68	2–2	0–0	0–0	0–0	2–2
Ritchie, W.	55–67	207–0	37–0	66–0	30–0	340–0
Roberts, G.	86–88	55–3	4–0	5–0	5–0	69–3
Robertson, C.	77–80	15–2	2–0	2–1	1–0	20–3
Robertson, D.	81–84	6–0	2–0	0–0	0–0	8–0
Robertson, S.	87–	3–0	0–0	0–0	0–0	3–0
Robertson, T.	57–58	0–0	0–0	1–0	0–0	1–0
Rodger, J.	53–55	3–0	0–0	0–0	0–0	3–0
Russell, R.	77–87	250–31	41–8	53–6	26–1	370–46
Rutherford, E.	46–52	95–19	17–4	28–5	0–0	140–28
Scott, Alex	54–63	216–68	25–5	62–23	28–12	331–108
Scott, Ally	73–76	35–10	4–2	15–7	0–0	54–19
Semple, W.	67–71	8–2	0–0	1–0	0–0	9–2
Setterington, D.	65–70	13–4	0–0	0–0	1–1	14–5
Sharp, R.	74–75	0–0	0–0	1–0	0–0	1–0
Shaw, Jock	46–53	169–1	27–0	42–0	0–0	238–1
Shaw, John	46–47	0–0	0–0	1–0	0–0	1–0
Shearer, R.	55–65	268–2	37–0	72–2	30–0	407–4
Simpson, R.	50–51	2–2	0–0	0–0	0–0	2–2
Simpson, W.	50–59	172–113	23–15	38–35	6–2	239–165
Smith, A.	66–69	41–20	2–0	14–5	11–1	68–26
Smith, D.	66–74	195–8	30–0	42–2	33–3	300–13
Smith, G.	77–80, 82–83	100–35	18–1	23–12	16–3	157–51
Smith, W.	56–58	2–0	0–0	0–0	0–0	2–0
Sorensen, E.	67–68	31–0	5–0	6–0	6–0	48–0
Sorensen, J.	65–66	12–3	4–0	0–0	0–0	16–3
Souness, G.	86–	50–3	5–0	9–2	9–0	73–5
Spackman, N.	89–	21–1	2–0	0–0	0–0	23–1
Stanners, D.	51–56	20–0	1–0	2–0	0–0	23–0
Stead, A.	46–47	3–0	0–0	1–1	0–0	4–1
Steele, J.	76–77	5–0	0–0	0–0	0–0	5–0
Stein, C.	68–72, 75–77	128–64	21–9	32–14	25–10	206–97
Sterland, M.	88–89	9–3	4–0	0–0	0–0	13–3
Steven, T.	89–	34–3	2–0	5–2	2–0	43–5
Stevens, Gary	88–	70–2	10–1	10–0	6–0	96–3
Stevens, Gregor	79–84	64–1	11–2	14–1	3–0	92–4
Stevenson, W.	58–62	73–1	12–0	9–0	9–0	103–1
Stewart, J.	80–84	56–0	9–0	21–0	6–0	92–0
Strickland, D.	77–79	1–0	0–0	1–0	0–0	2–0
Symon, S.	46–47	32–3	3–0	2–0	0–0	37–3
Telfer, W.	57–60	70–0	9–0	12–0	6–0	97–0
Thomson, A.	55–56	1–0	0–0	0–0	0–0	1–0
Thornton, W.	46–54	219–138	34–21	50–29	0–0	303–188
Traill, D.	63–66	4–0	1–0	0–0	0–0	5–0
Urquhart, W.	78–80	14–6	3–1	5–0	4–0	26–7
Valentine, J.	56–58	2–0	0–0	6–0	1–0	9–0
Vinnicombe, C.	89–	6–0	2–0	0–0	0–0	8–0
Waddell, W.	46–55	196–37	32–4	68–15	0–0	296–56
Walker, J.	56–57	2–0	0–0	0–0	0–0	2–0
Walker, N.	83–89	75–0	8–0	9–0	3–0	95–0
Walmsley, W.	48–49	1–0	0–0	0–0	0–0	1–0
Walters, M.	87–	76–20	12–5	10–10	4–1	102–36
Watkins, C.	46–48	9–0	1–0	3–0	0–0	13–0
Watson, C.	62–66	14–4	1–0	4–0	1–0	20–4
Watson, K.	69–71	4–0	0–0	0–0	0–0	4–0
Watson, K.	75–81	62–5	10–1	12–0	9–0	93–6
Watson, R.	64–70	51–4	11–2	14–1	6–0	82–7
Watson, R.M.	70–71	0–0	0–0	1–0	0–0	1–0
West, C.	86–87	10–2	1–0	2–1	2–0	15–3
White, W.	69–70	1–0	0–0	0–0	0–0	1–0
Wilkins, R.	87–89	70–2	9–0	10–1	7–0	96–3
Williamson, R.	83–87	41–12	4–2	5–6	2–0	52–20
Williamson, W.	46–51	43–24	9–7	17–8	0–0	69–39
Willougby, A.	62–69	74–39	3–1	11–6	5–1	93–47
Wilson, D.	56–67	227–97	38–21	71–27	37–10	373–155
Wood, W.	63–67	35–4	2–0	6–0	4–0	47–4
Woodburn, W.	46–55	216–1	38–0	71–0	0–0	325–1
Woods, C.	86–	137–0	12–0	16–0	16–0	181–0
Woods, J.	54–55	1–0	0–0	0–0	0–0	1–0
Woods, N.	86–88	3–0	0–0	0–0	0–0	3–0
Young, G.	79–81	2–0	0–0	0–0	0–0	2–0
Young, G.L.	46–57	293–22	50–5	83–4	2–0	428–31
Young, Q.	72–76	82–28	7–2	19–8	6–0	114–38